Routledge Revivals

Russia Forty Years On

First Published in 1961 *Russia Forty Years On* presents a comparative overview of Russian history from the Tsarist days to the Stalin Era. Morgan Philips Price looks back on Russia over a period of fifty years - the Tsarist time, the First World War, the October Revolution, and the time of Stalin; and describes his last visit there in the autumn of 1959. Though the book is mainly about Russia there are two chapters at the end about Germany and especially about that part which was under Russian influence. Having seen Russian Communism in its homeland, author compares it with what can be seen of it in Central Europe. This book will be an interesting read for scholars and researchers of Russian history, Communist history, and European history.

Russia Forty Years On
An account of a visit to Russia and Germany in the autumn of 1959

M. Philips Price

First published in 1961
by George Allen & Unwin Ltd

This edition first published in 2021 by Routledge
2 Park Square, Milton Park, Abingdon, Oxon, OX14 4RN
and by Routledge
605 Third Avenue, New York, NY 10017

Routledge is an imprint of the Taylor & Francis Group, an informa business

© George Allen & Unwin Ltd. 1961

All rights reserved. No part of this book may be reprinted or reproduced or utilised in any form or by any electronic, mechanical, or other means, now known or hereafter invented, including photocopying and recording, or in any information storage or retrieval system, without permission in writing from the publishers.

Publisher's Note
The publisher has gone to great lengths to ensure the quality of this reprint but points out that some imperfections in the original copies may be apparent.

Disclaimer
The publisher has made every effort to trace copyright holders and welcomes correspondence from those they have been unable to contact.

A Library of Congress record exists under LCCN: 61065880

ISBN: 978-1-032-15229-5(hbk)
ISBN: 978-1-003-24316-8(ebk)
ISBN: 978-1-032-15231-8(pbk)

Book DOI 10.4324/9781003243168

RUSSIA FORTY YEARS ON

*An account of a visit to Russia and
Germany in the autumn of* 1959

M. PHILIPS PRICE
M.A., F.R.G.S.

*With a chapter of impressions
by Mrs E. Price*

Ruskin House
GEORGE ALLEN & UNWIN LTD
MUSEUM STREET LONDON

FIRST PUBLISHED IN 1961

This book is copyright under the Berne Convention. Apart from any fair dealing for the purpose of private study, research, criticism or review, as permitted under the Copyright Act, 1956, no portion may be reproduced by any process without written permission. Enquiries should be addressed to the publisher.

© George Allen & Unwin Ltd, 1961

PRINTED IN GREAT BRITAIN
in 10 *on* 11 *point Plantin type*
BY T. & A. CONSTABLE LTD
HOPETOUN STREET, EDINBURGH

PREFACE

I FIRST went to Russia on a short visit in 1908 to see forests on the Finnish border. Having family interests in the timber trade and having had to do with commercial relations with Russia, I wanted to see something of her vast forest resources. In 1910 I was a member of a scientific expedition that explored the head waters of the Yenesei river on the borders of Siberia and Outer Mongolia and did the botanical and geological work for this expedition. On these trips I became acquainted with the great open spaces of Russia and saw something of the lives of her peasants and backwoodsmen. At the outbreak of the First World War, I went to Russia by arrangement with Mr C. P. Scott, the famous editor of the *Manchester Guardian*, a friend of my family, to report on Russia's war effort and to watch for any social changes that might come as a result of the war. In consequence, I came to be in Petrograd in the days of the October Revolution and got to meet Lenin. In 1945, when in Parliament for my home county where I was born, I went again to Russia after the victory over Hitler and saw the effects of the devastation and the beginnings of the Stalin era. On retiring from Parliament last autumn I went back there again to see the country under the milder régime of Mr Krushchev. This time my wife came with me. Because of these visits, I was able to compare the Russia of today with what I remember of Tsarist days, the First World War, the October Revolution and the Stalin era—a span of from forty years to half a century.

As an old Harrovian my thoughts have often gone back to that greatest of all school songs 'Forty Years On'. Hence the title of this book. In the words of the song, 'God gives us bases to guard or beleaguer', and I felt that He had given me a base to guard, namely to try and preserve the memories of what I had seen in one of the great revolutions of history and of the passing of a great and talented people through a terrible ordeal from an antiquated society into the modern world.

But in this book I cannot do more than give sketches of the past or, as my old school song says, record 'Glimpses of notes like the catch of a song' which came to me as I looked on scenes of Russia today and remembered what I had once known. A fuller account will come later, but I feel I must make some contribution now in view of the tension over Russia.

My wife's contribution is very different from mine, but I am sure in some ways more interesting. For she was born and brought up in the harsh atmosphere of post-Bismarckian Prussia. But having lived in Berlin and having been in the working class and Socialist

Preface

movement of that unattractive city of sturdy independence, she is sufficiently Western in her outlook to have been rather shocked at the unconventionality of the Russian way of life, for she had never been there before. What caused her to raise her eyebrows at some of what she saw in Russia, left me cold. For I had known my Russia and seen all this before. It was all part of that somewhat shocking, attractive, slap-dash nature of a people who are at once crude, able and very lovable to those who know them.

Anyone who goes to Russia today and then writes about his experiences should be especially careful to do all he can to cool down the antagonism that has developed between Russia and the Western countries since the Second World War. But we must face facts. This antagonism is not of recent date. It is centuries old. Though they have only once led to war between Russia and the West in the Crimea, there have been prolonged periods of tension, and on the three occasions when the West were allied with Russia, first against Napoleon in last and then against Germany in this century, the alliances have been short-lived. It looks as if the German wars at any rate have only been episodes in the much more fundamental antagonism between the Eurasian continental autocracies and the democracies of the West.

But to understand the reason for and nature of this antagonism is a vital problem for all of us, for the fate of mankind may depend on it. I try to show in this book how different the history and traditions of Russia are to ours. Autocratic and centralized forms of government have been a historical necessity for Russia, who has never had the long education in democratic systems like we, the French and the Americans have had. The antagonism is really deep-seated. It can be traced back originally to the hostility between the nomadic people of the steppes of Central Asia under their autocratic rulers and the free maritime peoples of the Mediterranean and Atlantic seaboards. This was first noticed as far back as the fifth century B.C., by the 'Father of History', Herodotus, when he describes the life and death struggles between Greece and Persia. The USSR is the inheritor of the original autocratic power in Central Asia which culminated in the Mongol invasion of Europe in the thirteenth century. It has continued the tradition of that régime through the Tsardom of Muscovy. Tribes living in desert steppes, open to attack on all sides, never feel safe and so submit to autocratic rulers to protect themselves. Sea-going people on the other hand, trading with the world, feel safer and freer. Hence this age-long antagonism, which has for centuries been fought out along the periphery of Eastern Europe, between the peoples of Central and Western Asia and the peoples of the Western seacoasts.

Preface

The conflict has taken various forms. After the Graeco-Persian there was the Roman-Parthian conflict. Then there was the incursion of the Huns into South-East Europe early in the Christian era. Then there was the struggle that went on for many decades between the Ottoman Empire under its great Sultans and the Holy Roman Empire, for the Turks were originally nomads from Central Asia. After the Mongol invasion, the Tsars of Muscovy began to consolidate power and to acquire the traditional form of autocratic government from their former overlords, the Mongols. There followed the wars between Peter the Great and Sweden, the struggle over and partition of Poland, the rivalry between the Russian and Austrian Empires over the Balkans and over the fragments breaking away from the now declining Ottoman Empire. An East-West struggle is not a thing of today or even of yesterday. It is age-old and it is fascinating to see from records of the past what fear has been engendered in the minds of people of all types in Western Europe as the rising power of Russia began, after the seventeenth century, to replace the older autocracies of Asia. It is also interesting to see what Russians from time to time have thought of themselves and of their rôle in Europe. I have made it my business from time to time to collect quotations of this kind and I refer readers to the Appendix at the end of this book. Some of the sayings of Russians about their Messianic mission in Europe might have been written by Russian Communists during the October Revolution. It is on all fours with what the Abbot Theophilus of Pskov wrote to Tsar Basil III in 1547 about Moscow and the Third Rome.

We are all in fear now that this new East-West antagonism may lead in the scientific age of today to World War III and the destruction of mankind. I have been mindful of this all through these pages and I have noted and shown that this fear is not confined to us, but affects the Russians too. I have tried to show how, as the memory of the great October Revolution recedes into the background, the people of the USSR seem increasingly interested in other things than the spreading of Communism about the world by forceful means. The implication of what I have written is that, given time, the cooling process in Russia will go on and the age-long antagonism between Central Asia and the maritime people of Western Europe will fade out. But we, too, have a share of responsibility to say and do nothing to stop this process in Russia. A false move, a hasty action may plunge us into disaster. Time is wanted for this cooling process which follows all great revolutions. But firmness and unity is also wanted in the West or the Russians will today, as in the past, exploit weaknesses.

The comparisons which I have given in these pages between the Russia that I once knew and the Russia that I now see show me, and

Preface

I hope the reader, that the process of cooling down is going on and that everything must be done to foster understanding between East and West without the West abandoning its way of life any more than the Russians need abandon their way.

We returned from Russia over land via East and West Germany. Here again I was able to make comparisons with the past, Germany of today with the Germany that I remembered between 1919 and 1923, nearly forty years ago. I had gone to Germany at the end of 1918 direct from Russia after the collapse of the Hohenzollern régime, when the Bolsheviks in Russia were convinced that the World Revolution had begun and Germany was to be the first state to go Communist after them. I lived through the long period of disillusionment both for the Russian Communists and for Democratic and Republican Germany which ended, after I had left Germany, in the disaster of Hitler.

My wife and I visited Berlin, both the East and West parts of the city, where we saw some things that reminded us of the past and some that pointed to new values that had never been in old Germany. Fortunately also we were able to get permission to visit the East Zone of Germany and to see the old town of Halberstadt, where my wife was born and lived the first fourteen years of her life. We describe our reception there and the reaction of the people to the alien Communist régime. Looking back over nearly forty years, I was able to see that the German people had suffered in no way less than the Russian people during that time. But the defeat of Germany in the Second World War, the collapse of all government and the foreign occupation has prevented Germany from going forward united and has resulted in disunion and the partition of the country into two separate types of civilization.

Germany is politically one of the youngest countries in Europe, with, however, a very old culture. But Germany in the past has had two souls, one seeking attachment to the democratic West and the other to the autocratic East. The latter was derived in Bismarck's day from contact with Tsarist Russia and its theocratic tradition, the former stems from the inspiration of the French Revolution. The two German wars of this century have been the struggle to exorcise the first of these souls. As I show in the two chapters at the end of this book, this has only taken place in West Germany. The East remains under a peculiarly truculent form of Communism which is declining in Russia itself but now is galvanizing the partition of Germany. Though very different socially and economically from the Prussian junker and military system of the past, it is one with it in its undemocratic and autocratic political system. There is little sign of any change yet.

CONTENTS

PREFACE   page 7

    I   *Finnish Approaches*   15

   II   *Leningrad*   20

  III   *Moscow (Part I)*   36

  IV   *Moscow (Part II)*   52

   V   *Kieff and the Ukraine*   64

  VI   *Agriculture and the Ukrainian Village*   77

 VII   *Berlin Past and Present*   89

VIII   *A Visit to East Germany*   102

  IX   *A Woman's Impressions of Russia and a Visit to Former Childhood Scenes in Germany (By Mrs E. Price)*   110

Appendix   123

INDEX   128

ILLUSTRATIONS

1. Timber Port at St Petersburg   *facing page* 32
   Timber Port at Leningrad

2. Leningrad—Fortress of Peter and Paul   33
   Leningrad—Smolny Institute and statue of Lenin

3. Moscow—Cathedral of the Assumption   48
   Moscow—Kremlin gardens with Mrs Price and guide

4. Moscow—the new university   49
   Kieff—public park

5. Kieff—River Dnieper   80
   Country house of Polish aristocrat (1915)

6. Ukrainian peasants and retainers (1915)   81
   Collective Farm in Ukraine; house for public gatherings

7. Collective Farm: cattle shed   96
   Collective Farm: our host and family

8. Collective Farm in North Russia   97
   Collective Farm in Kazakistan

CHAPTER I

THE FINNISH APPROACHES

On a Russian steamer in the Baltic; types of passengers; arrival in Helsinki; memories of the Russian Baltic fleet; memories of the Revolution; Russo-Finnish comradeship is tinged with suspicion; how Helsinki has changed; memories of demonstrations before the Finnish Diet; a visit to a graveyard and the victims of former wars; Russo-Finnish relations today.

MY wife and I were sitting in the saloon of the Russian passenger steamer *Baltika* sailing eastwards across the Baltic. Dinner was over and the passengers were chatting in groups. There were tables for cards and part of the floor had been cleared for dancing. There were parties of English people going out on short tourist trips arranged by Intourist (the official Russian Travel Agency) for a week or ten days in Leningrad and Moscow. No very great impression can be got on such a trip, but Russian travel is expensive and that is better than nothing. Anyway, it is better than in Stalin's day, when no one could go at all.

But what interested me was not my countrymen going to Russia, but Russians returning from my country. There were quite a number of them. Some were young diplomats going on leave, some were representatives of State Trusts who had been doing business, buying or selling, in Britain. But then there were tourists as well, and they interested me most of all. Here at last were Russian citizens who had been out of their country and visiting the free West, also for a week or ten days. They had some leader who, no doubt, was 'reliable', but they seemed singularly free in their expressions of opinion and in their general talk. One party of about ten had been to London, Coventry and Manchester. They were not university students, but people already commencing their careers. One was doing a post-graduate course in engineering, another had completed a course at the Musical Conservatory in Moscow and was taking a teaching job, a third was a librarian in a provincial town. Money had been found for the journey and they all belonged to some professional society which had sponsored their trip, but most of them seemed to have contributed something from their salaries as well. They were highly delighted at having been in England and genuinely seemed to have enjoyed themselves. They were also impressed with what they had seen. It seemed to have confirmed what they had expected—a country where people were on the whole well-off, where things were not organized at the top so much as in Russia, and yet everything seemed to work. One young woman who was learning to play the organ thought a lot of the organ at Manchester Cathedral. Others were impressed with the public parks in London. As if in return for what they had seen, they wanted to advise me what to see and look for in Russia. When I told them that I had first visited Russia in Tsarist times fifty years ago when I was quite a young man and had been in Leningrad during the Revolution, my stock went up considerably. Then I must compare Russia today with what I remembered of Russia under the old régime, they said. That, I said, was just why I was coming to Russia. We must travel and see each others' countries more, they said. But surely you people think that you don't need to learn anything and that your way of doing things is the best in the world, I asked facetiously? It is the best for Russia, they said, but each people must do what is best for them. There were certainly no preconceived Marxist doctrines among these Russian tourists. Yet they were good, patriotic Russians.

It was nine o'clock. One young woman sat down at the piano. Others of the Russian parties got round her. The tunes of Russian folk-songs began to float on the air. Whenever and wherever Russians are gathered together round a piano, a guitar or an accordion, there is soon music to be heard. And soon after music comes dancing. The urge for music and dancing is inherent in the Russian character. From the dance-halls of Moscow to remote Siberian village greens, it is all the same. An untranslatable Russian word 'sobornost' means, perhaps, the 'state of living together'.[1] That is the essence of Russian society. I remember experiencing it in far-off days when I first went to Russia half a century ago. In spite of revolution, civil war, Hitler's war and the coming of the 'sputnik', it is still there today. It was there on that Russian ship ploughing its way eastwards across the Baltic. Folk-songs and snatches from the operas of Glinka, Pushkin and Tschaikowsky rang through the saloon till far into the night.

Next morning we were entering the channel leading to the port and city of Helsinki, the capital of Finland. We were already on the threshold of Eastern Europe and near that indefinable line that separates it from the West. Yet there was Helsinki with its Lutheran churches and its silent, stubborn people. This was not yet the East. It was here that Russians and Finns had made contact over the centuries. Once part of the great northern empire of Sweden, Finland has gradually, since Peter the Great's day, fallen under

[1] The Americans have coined a word 'togetherness' which might cover it.

Russian influence but has managed to keep its identity. For the Russian influence has been rather superficial. As the *Baltika* steamed through a narrow channel into a wider bay, I remembered seeing once the greater part of the Russian Baltic fleet riding at anchor here. That was after the fall of the Tsar and during the Kerensky period when the liberal elements thrown up by the March Revolution were trying to build up a democratic régime of a Western European type. But the Finns were suspicious and frightened. Here was this Russian Baltic fleet overshadowing the Finnish capital. It was there because of a treaty with a Tsar now gone. The Finns looked East and saw a red glare in the sky and heard the cry 'Workers of the world unite!' and they trembled. As our ship passed the spot where I had seen the Baltic fleet riding at anchor, I remembered having gone from the old fortress of Sveaborg in a launch lent me by the Russian Soviet of Sailors' Deputies to visit some of the ships. Near that island had floated the battleship *Petropavlovsk*. I had been received there by the marines, who had arrested their officers and were running the ship. They had all been members of the Socialist-revolutionary party but they had just passed a resolution declaring for the Communists, then called Bolsheviks. As for the destroyers, rumour had it that they had just gone over to the Anarchists! There certainly was anarchy in the Baltic fleet when, forty-three years ago, I had last been there and seen Russia in dissolution and Finland struggling to get free.

Yet I remember many acts of comradeship among Russians and Finns in those days. I looked for and thought I recognized a little island in the bay outside Helsinki. Here I had gone with a party of Russian sailors and Finnish Social Democrats one day in July 1917. They were going to do homage to the memory of some Russian sailors whose graves were there. They had been condemned to death and executed by Tsarist gendarmes for the part they had played in the revolt of the Russian Baltic fleet and of the garrison of the fortress of Sveaborg in the abortive Revolution of 1905. We landed on the island and walked solemnly to the graves, Russians and Finns in silent sorrow for what had happened twelve years ago. Then one of the Russian sailors, who had been an eye-witness, described how the sailors were tied to stakes while grim, grey-coated gendarmes did their work. The Russian revolutionary dirge for fallen comrades was then sung and the Finns joined in as best they could. Then all filed past the graves back to the boats, and from many eyes, both Russian and Finnish, tears rolled silently down.

Our steamer landed at the port and we went on shore for several hours. The business quarters of Helsinki were buzzing with activity, multiple shops were crowded, restaurants full. In the square outside the main railway station I remembered a number of rather *de luxe* hotels. They were all gone now and in their place were business premises and Government offices. If there are any very rich people today in Finland, they are not in evidence in the capital. There were extensive areas outside the city where I remembered beaches and forested shores, but not a house. These are now covered with villas and bungalows of the middle and professional classes. There they keep their yachts and bathe and sail at week-ends. Society has apparently become in these forty years much less polarized between rich and poor, even in a country where the Communists are only a minority.

I went to the large square where stands the Lutheran cathedral. On one side are Government buildings. On the other side there used to be a building where the Finnish Diet once met, now it is used for something else. My mind went back to a great gathering of Russian sailors of the Baltic fleet, soldiers from the Russian garrison stationed in Finland and some Finnish workers from the factories. They met in that square on the steps of the cathedral in July 1917. A Bill was being discussed in the Diet that day to extend the franchise which had hitherto been weighted in favour of property. I remembered seeing a huge Russian sailor with a voice like the last trumpet, speaking and saying to his brother soldiers and sailors: 'Come, comrades, let us go to the Diet and sing them a fine song.' So they all marched to the Diet and sang Russian revolutionary songs outside it. But the Finnish workers hung back and took no part and the Finnish passers-by looked on the Russians coldly. Russian intervention in internal Finnish affairs was not wanted. Yet my impression at the time was that the Russians were quite genuine and had a warm-hearted and generous desire to help the Finns. It never occurred to them that the Finns might think differently. The Russians were thinking in terms of international revolutionary socialism; the Finns, apparently all classes of them, were thinking in terms of national self-determination. Here was the beginning of trouble, and I had seen it that day in 1917.

My wife and I then joined a party of passengers from the ship to see the sights of Helsinki. And among other things we saw the cemetery of war graves on the edge of the city. Round a clock tower in forested surroundings were acres and acres of graves. I looked to see in what war or wars the men had died and found that the inscriptions revealed the tragic course of Finnish history. There were the graves of those who, a century and a half ago, had fought in a confused struggle between the Russian Emperor Alexander and the King of Sweden first on one side, then on the other. Then in another part were the graves of those who had fought with Germany against Russia under General Mannerheim after the October Revolution. Finnish nationalism had overcome any urge that some may have had to join their great revolutionary neighbour in the East. The comradeship of those Russian sailors and Finnish citizens who mourned the victims of Tsarism on the little island where I had been in July 1917, had faded. The suspicion of the Finns for those sailors who demonstrated before the Finnish Diet had won the day. And most tragic of all, there were the graves of Finns who had died fighting for Hitler and helping him to blockade and starve Leningrad in the Second World War.

Finland has retained her independence to this day and the Russians still harbour a healthy respect for those sturdy, stubborn people who will not join their boisterous eastern neighbour, but who also realize that that neighbour is too big and strong now to defy and must be lived with. I found among Russians whom I met in Helsinki and later in Moscow that co-operation in economic affairs between Finland and Russia is close and that the occupation of Finnish strategic points on the Gulf of Finland is made with as little display as possible and is being steadily reduced. As our ship sailed out of Helsinki harbour eastwards towards the real Iron Curtain, I felt that Russians and Finns have found, after a stormy past, a way of living together as good neighbours in spite of very great differences.

CHAPTER II

LENINGRAD

Arrival in Leningrad; first impressions; talks with the people in queues; prices in the shops; unattractive housing conditions; I visit my old haunts and have memories of the Revolution; I visit Leningrad's timber port; St Isaacs; visit to churches; visit to the Peter and Paul Fortress; the Tsars' dungeons; Peter the Great and his work; Lenin and his work; we visit the Smolny Institute and I have memories of the October Revolution; I visit old haunts at the Taurida Palace; place where I once saw Lenin face a critical situation single-handed; Leningrad opera; Leningrad art galleries; Russian and Western art side by side.

IN due course the *Baltika* steamed up the channel from the Gulf of Finland into the new and spacious port of Leningrad. We were met at the quay by a representative of the Russian Travel Agency (Intourist) who had everything perfectly arranged for us. A guide and interpreter is provided as part of the service for which you pay. In my case no interpreter was necessary, but it was an advantage to have someone to pass you through the formalities and, as we later found, to arrange appointments by telephone for meeting people and arranging interviews. Moreover, my wife spoke no Russian, and if we went to different places in one day, an interpreter was needed for her. The impression I got with the passport control officials and with the customs was that they must have had orders to make the visits of foreign tourists as easy as possible. There was no inspection of literature, and I had a fair number of books and periodicals with me, and so had my wife. But nothing was looked at. I had not got *Dr Zhivago* with me, as I had already read it! The most formidable literary work that my wife had was Tolstoy's *War and Peace*, as popular now in the Soviet Union as it was in the days of the Tsar.

Having got settled in the Astoria Hotel in the square, opposite the great cathedral of St Isaacs, I began to look around. I went about by myself while my wife was resting. If you did not want the interpreter or guide, you could go off by yourself, and, as far as I could see, no one seemed to follow me. The last time I had seen Leningrad was not long after the Second World War. The scars of that terrible encounter were all there and the suburbs on the south of the city were a shambles. The centre had been quickly restored and looked as it did in the days of the Tsar. Now even the suburbs bore no scars of the war and Leningrad looked very much as I had known it over forty years ago, with the exception of one area to which I shall refer later. But the atmosphere was not the same. When I first knew it, it was the capital of the Empire. There was an official atmosphere about it. Everyone was very busy and rather reserved. Most people seemed to be keeping appointments, attending conferences and had little time to talk to strangers. That atmosphere seemed to transmit itself even to the small businesses and shops.

In those days it was called St Petersburg and no one was afraid of speaking German or even of boasting of the German efficiency which to some extent permeated the Russian capital as it had done ever since the days of Peter the Great. Then came the First World War and everything German had to be erased. The city assumed the pure Slavonic name of Petrograd, which means the same as Petersburg but was more patriotic. German businesses were closed down and the press was full of articles about 'niemetsky zasil' (German domination) over Russia. No one seemed to know just what the domination consisted of, but the phrase served its purpose for the time. Then came the Revolution, and after the second one in October 1917 the Soviet régime decided to make Moscow the capital once more. Moscow was further from the West and Germany really was a menace now, having occupied Riga and penetrated into the Baltic provinces of the old Empire. So I remember leaving Petrograd in one of the few crowded trains to Moscow at the end of February 1918, and when I next came back it was called Leningrad, after that great man who had led and guided the October Revolution during the early phases of its heroic struggles—Lenin. By that time Leningrad was a provincial city once more, as it had been till the end of the seventeenth century before Peter's day. The bustle, the coolness and the preoccupation of the people had now transferred itself to Moscow and Leningrad was human once more. I noticed that when I was there in 1946 and again now.

For instance, soon after arrival I decided to go out by myself and wander about the Nevsky Prospect, visiting the shops in the arcade near the former Kazan cathedral. I wanted some apples, and in a side-street I came across some fruit stalls where quite a queue had formed. I got into it and soon got into conversation with the men and women near me. My accent betrayed me, although when I lived in Russia people used to mistake me for a Baltic German, for whom Russian is the second native tongue after German. Anyway, I informed them that I was British and instantly about half a dozen people got round me. They wanted to know what life was like in

England, what were the prices of things, how much did people earn a month at their various jobs. One woman told me that her coat for the winter had cost her 1,200 roubles and was hardly warm enough for the cold spells. How does that compare with prices in England, I was asked? I had to do some mental arithmetic and informed them that, at the official rate of exchange between the pound and the rouble, that coat would cost about £100. But at the more realistic tourist rate which I was getting (30 roubles to the pound) that would be £40. So I told them that, and said that a coat like that in England would cost about £15. 'Well,' said one man, 'I hope that Krushchev will now be able to make things better through more trade with other countries in Europe.' (Krushchev was at this time visiting America.) In general, there were appreciative remarks about Krushchev, who was clearly popular on the grounds that he was thought to be trying to improve the lot of the Soviet citizen.

I went on to the arcade near the former Kazan cathedral on the Nevsky Prospect. This used to be the place where fashionable St Petersburg did its shopping. Now there are the stalls of the Consumers' Co-operatives and the State Trusts (G.U.M.), for there are no private shops now. There was plenty in the shops, but the prices were high relative to prices in the free world of Western Europe. A pair of low-heeled shoes for men and women were from 200 to 250 roubles. At the tourist rate of exchange, that would be £8. The same kind of shoes with us would cost about £3. Women's hats of poor quality were from £5 to £7, at the tourist rate, but no woman would be seen in such hats in France or England. A poor evening-dress which with us would be about £10 was marked at £20 at the tourist rate. On the other hand, a wireless set was about the same price as with us. Here, no doubt, good Russian technical work has brought the price down, but, as I shall show later, the use of these instruments is not as great as with us. People I got talking to here were quite open in telling me what they earned. Many earned 600 roubles a month and some up to 1,000. That would be at the tourist rate £20 a month or £5 a week, and £33 a month or £8 a week respectively. But wages and salaries were coming in to the families often through both husband and wife and sometimes through a son. So the family income might easily be £15 a week or even £20. Rent of flats is fantastically cheap and all are run by the municipality. One had the impression that wages and salaries did not compare unfavourably with the West, but against that, these earnings were being eaten into more than in the West by high consumers' goods prices. What is the cause of all this? I will refer to this in later chapters.

But meanwhile the lasting impression I got from my street and shop talks with the common people of Leningrad was that the people had no fear of talking to foreigners. There was no looking over their shoulder to see if anyone is listening. People say what they think and are most friendly to foreigners. The Russians, being talkative and sociable people, feel it rather a compliment when a foreigner comes and goes about among them. This again is as it used to be when I first knew Russia. The Revolution, like all revolutions, produces its terror which, however, passes. They had at one time to keep their mouths shut, for it is always an authoritarian state where the executive and the police have great power, but apparently less than they had. Clearly since Stalin's death, Krushchev has been gradually letting up on freedom of speech and no one is really afraid now as they were till recently. In any case the impression one gets is that the Soviet régime is not unpopular, that the Russians are a patriotic people with great love of their way of life and their outlook on things and there seems to be a general feeling that the Government is doing the best it can for them. Another impression one gets is that food is plentiful and cheap. This particularly applies to butter. Compared with fourteen years ago when I was there last, this is a great improvement. The poor quality and high prices are almost entirely in durable and non-durable consumers' goods of general use.

One is struck by the extremely poor styles of dress and standards of personal appearances. We found this in all the places we visited. This rather shocked my wife, but did not shock me, for forty or fifty years ago when I first knew Russia, it was exactly the same. The only well-dressed people then were the members of the aristocracy and the higher bureaucracy. They dressed like Parisians. Now they have disappeared in the Revolution and the people go on as before, with no apparent desire to look nice. The high price of clothes and footwear is not entirely the cause of this. The people of Poland are even worse off in many ways as regards quality of consumers' goods and prices. Yet the Poles, particularly the women, have a great flair for dress and appearances and on next to nothing still look extremely nice. In Russia, men and women slouch about in clothes that look like sacks, and the figure is completely absent, camouflaged partly through the enormous quantities of bread and potatoes eaten. One thing, however, I liked. Russia is saved from the fantastic fashions of the West in women's dress. Particularly I was glad to see the absence of the very high-heeled shoes.

I said above that the scars of war in Leningrad had been removed and that the city looks much as it did when I first knew it. That is not quite correct. There are areas which, if not war-scarred, look virtually derelict. They looked poor when I knew them first. They look more neglected now, as if the population has declined or the City Council has not thought it worth while to keep the houses in repair. Of course, it has been the general policy since the attack of Hitler on Russia to shift major industries away from the western region towards the Urals and Siberia. Actually, Lenin originated the move soon after the October Revolution. This resulted in a decline of the population of Leningrad, although in recent years it has remained about stable. The main economic activities of Leningrad are the industries connected with the Russian export trade, especially in timber, pulp wood, ship-repairing and ship-building, and general international commerce, including the import from abroad of machinery. Though the Kiroff works (formerly Putiloff) continue to function, large new engineering works are discouraged and the State Trusts tend to site their industries farther east.

Consequently, one sees some dismal areas in Leningrad. One is on the Vassily Island and the old 'Petersburg' suburb. My wife and I were being taken by an Intourist guide to see the new stadium which, it is hoped, may one day attract the Olympic Games. It is the show thing for foreigners to see. But Intourist should really be more careful. It does not impress foreigners when, in order to reach this fine stadium, they have to pass for some ten minutes through streets of houses and flats which clearly have had no paint since the nineteen-thirties, where the plaster is falling off, where windows are broken and apparently never mended. Enquiries into whose job it was to mend broken windows elicited the reply that it was no one's job particularly and that it was largely left to the tenants. Anyway there seemed to be a general atmosphere of decay pervading that part of Leningrad.

A little later that day we went to another part of the city near the centre. On one of the canals coming from the Neva is the so-called Fontanka near the Winter Gardens, with its marble figures of Greek gods and heroes who figure in the first scene of Pushkin's 'Queen of Spades'. Here in number 18, back off the street and overlooking what was once quite a nice courtyard, was the flat where I rented a room in 1917 and early 1918. It was here that I lived during the exciting days of the October Revolution and where, after returning home tired and hungry from hearing and reporting about the meetings of the All-Russia Soviet Congress, I had to stay up most of the night with fellow-tenants in the other flats to guard the main gateway to prevent drunken soldiers from getting into our precincts. Shots were being fired and wine-cellars in a neighbouring street had been broken into and things generally looked ugly for some nights. I looked at the doors on the Fontanka along the canal where I used to shelter from bullets when I was finding my way home, running from door to door during periods of lull in the firing. That was when, for three days and three nights, the Kronstadt sailors from across the canal were besieging the Red Fort, the old red building which was the Military Academy and where some hundred or more cadets, loyal to the Kerensky régime, were holding out and resisting.

I went inside and found my flat. It was derelict and apparently uninhabited. Some creepers had grown over the windows, which were dim with dust. Inside the room I had cooked for myself meagre meals till food virtually gave out and I had to live on one quarter-pound of sour, black rye-bread a day and a smoked herring which by merciful providence one could buy from barrows on the banks of the Neva. The herrings came from the Murman coast many hundred miles to the north in the Arctic Circle, and I never found out how they were brought in. But I think they saved my life. I looked into the derelict flat. I remembered a bath that I had in tepid water with freezing weather outside, when I looked at myself and almost burst into tears, for I was so weak. For I saw myself virtually a skeleton. I managed to weigh myself and found I was eight stone, my normal weight being twelve stone. The lights used to go out at ten o'clock each night to economize on electric current, so when I was not doing guard-duty on the main gate I had to spend all night in darkness till the sun rose about eight o'clock.

Looking back on those days, I realized that I had indeed suffered with the Russian people in their great struggle for freedom and a new life which, however, so tantalizingly eluded them even after all their sufferings. But I had been sustained by the feeling that, even if I should not come through that period alive, something great was happening which I ought to see and report on for my newspaper; and the fact is that it was, as Charles James Fox said of the French Revolution, 'The greatest thing that had happened in the history of the world.' I remembered after the Cadets in the Red Fort had been captured and shot by the Kronstadt sailors and there was no more firing along the canal, I was able to get out and visit the Smolny Institute where the Soviet Congress was in session. I walked for a time and then weakness overcame me and I had to sit down and wait for the number 18 tram which at intervals of half an hour rolled along. I looked at the places in the street where I used to sit down on doorsteps and wait for that tram. That part of Leningrad where I had lived, though not as derelict as parts that I saw on the Vassily Island, had also pockets of decay. Not as many people now live in the centre of the city and new blocks of flats and housing schemes are in the southern suburbs, many of them excellent buildings.

I was asked to go down to visit the timber port of Leningrad. I am director of a family timber business and our firm has for many decades, in fact since the days of my grandfather, imported timber from Russia. I have a copy of a letter written by my grandfather to

Lord Clarendon, the Foreign Minister in Lord Palmerston's Government, asking permission to get the timber which he had bought out of the port of Archangel, which was being blockaded by the British Navy, for the Crimean War had begun and we were at war with Russia. I have not got the answer, but I doubt if my grandfather got his timber till after the war.

The Leningrad representative of the State Timber Export Trust ('Exportles') had been informed of my coming and sent a car to take me down to their offices in the docks. The little man who had been appointed as a guide to my wife and myself heard that I was going down to the timber yards and immediately developed a great desire to go with me. I told him that it was not necessary and that I knew the language, but he thought I should be accompanied down there. The official who had been sent to meet me asked me if I knew who the young man was. I told him and said that he wanted to come too. The official went off and talked to the young man away from me and evidently said something to him, and the young man went off with his tail between his legs and did not show himself till next day. This was a very revealing incident, for it showed how Soviet Government officials sometimes treat people who are obviously members of the Communist Party and who poke their noses into affairs that do not concern them. No doubt Intourist has to have its guides and interpreters from either the Communist Party members or from people who are vetted by the Party. But they can apparently get put in their places, for many, if not most, Government officials are not members of the Party.

So I went down to the timber port and was shown round. There were acres and acres of beautifully prepared, seasoned and stacked pine and spruce deals (Red and Whitewood). I saw the ships being loaded and preparing to sail to Britain, Western Europe, the Mediterranean and West Africa with Russian timber. All the latest machinery for lifting large heaps of timber and for moving them to the ship was there. Some of the machines were operated by women, who also were doing a certain amount of deal carrying and working on the timber piles. I talked with some of them. They were hardy and tough. One was earning an equivalent of £6 a week at the tourist rate of exchange and her husband was earning 1,000 roubles, making a total of £15 a week. They had no children as yet, she told me, but they were saving up in order to be able to afford to have some. There is no doubt these people work hard, but they are now assisted by various welfare organizations who help them when they have children.

I was able to take photographs of the timber yards but not of the ships being loaded. Then I was asked into the office for drinks. They told me how they regarded their timber as the largest single raw material export for earning foreign currency for Russia and they were anxious to expand their trade, especially with Britain. They were bringing their timber in by rail and river from Karelia on the borders of Finland, Vologda in the centre of North Russia and as far east as Viatka. There was an atmosphere of the utmost friendliness towards me and a readiness to tell me anything I wanted. One gets the impression that the Soviet Government are going all out to expand their foreign trade with all countries, and not the least with the countries of Western Europe. They need foreign currency because they appear to value certain machinery made in Germany, Britain, Belgium and France and also in America. They are not prepared to spend their gold, which they keep for emergencies, and so they earn it in this way. There seems to be some difficulty in foreseeing what they will have to export because all foreign trade is nationalized and decisions are centralized in Moscow, and the huge bureaucratic machine takes weeks and even months to come to a decision. So the Timber Trust often does not know until the last minute of an exporting season what it can export. Russia, of course, has not been able to export so much in proportion to her population as she used to because, owing to the enormous industrial development in the country, the consumption of food and raw material which is normally exported has enormously increased within the country. Very little grain is now exported, and the export of timber is less than it was. But they are trying to increase the output, and there is no doubt that Russian timber can be the best on the market, though it can also be the worst, because the machinery of production and distribution does not function as effectively or as efficiently as in the old timber-exporting countries of Sweden and Finland.

In Leningrad there is nothing in architecture to remind one of the old Russia of the pre-Petrine era. Even the Orthodox churches might have been taken from the Rome of the Renaissance period. Also the functions of many of these churches have changed. For instance, the St Isaac's cathedral, built like St Peter's at Rome, is a museum of ecclesiastical art and architecture. In keeping with the new scientific and secular age there is also an interesting demonstration of a pendulum suspended from the gigantic roof indicating the fact that the world revolves by showing the deviation of the course of the pendulum from the straight line. In the Kazan cathedral, also built like St Peter's at Rome, there is a museum indicating the history of religion from the earliest times. It is quite objective and not repugnant to an Orthodox Christian, but it does try to show that religion is only a phase in the evolution of Man's thinking and that he is growing out of it.

Yet no one need think that the old Russian faith does not exist. When Sunday came, I enquired from our Intourist guide where there was a church service going on. I was told that the service was now over. As it was only nine o'clock, I knew this could not be so, so we found out just where the nearest functioning church was and my wife and I went there. We found a quite large church, fairly modern and not very beautiful, but packed to the roof. Moreover, there were two services going on, one on an upper storey where a sermon was being preached on the value of prayer; and one on a lower storey where the mass was being sung. There must have been at least two thousand people on the two storeys and there were people of all ages and sexes there. This church served an area of Leningrad and there was every reason to suppose that there were similar churches in other parts of the city, but owing to the fact that the churches had to be supported by the people entirely now and not by large ecclesiastical endowments as once upon a time, there are naturally fewer churches than there used to be. But they seem more crowded than ever. So much for the veracity of some of the Intourist guides. I ought to say, however, that this sort of thing is not true of all of them. The one in Leningrad whom we had was evidently a member of the Communist Party, and not a very intelligent one at that. Others we had in other places were quite different, most tolerant and helpful in the matter of churches.

Next day, my wife and I went to look at the church called 'Na Krovi', built over the spot where the Emperor Alexander II was assassinated. On the canal embankment outside is a sacred ikon. I remembered it from former times. It was still there and, what is more, is still the object of veneration, for while we were there we watched a young woman making her devotions most fervently before it.

Yet Leningrad is, and has been for two and a half centuries, a monument to a new Russia. For Peter the Great was a great innovator and his work is seen everywhere. Not least of all it is to be seen in the Fortress of Peter and Paul, that forbidding bastion on the Neva, where the later Tsars imprisoned their 'politicals' and where many revolutionaries were done to death. Today one is taken round to see these dismal dungeons with hardly any light in them, where human beings were incarcerated for years. I remembered being there in November 1917, just after the October Revolution, and having interviewed some of the former Tsar's ministers, among them the notorious General Sukhumlinoff, the War Minister of Nicholas II. He had a lot to do with sparking off the First World War by mobilizing the Russian Army before any other of the Great Powers mobilized theirs and then lying to the Emperor about having done so. I also had seen some of Kerensky's junior ministers there. They had put Sukhumlinoff and other Tsarist ministers and generals into the fortress and then, within six months, were there themselves, having been 'Caliphs of the Hour'!

Across the Neva, near the canal separating the fortress from the mainland, is the wooden hut where Peter the Great lived while directing the work of founding out of a swamp the city that bore his name. Across the water on the southern shore were the majestic palaces (now mostly museums and Government offices) built by Peter. It was all in Italian style and is not unfittingly called sometimes the Venice of the North. Yet how often in Russian history have great things been done in ruthless ways. These great palaces and buildings were only built on solid land because of the slave labour, often resulting in death and maiming, of many thousand Russian peasants. One could not help thinking of this when looking at the wonderful sight of Leningrad from the Fortress of Peter and Paul. Whenever great volcanic changes take place in Russia even today, human life is sacrificed. But the people of Russia are inured to suffering, which shows itself in much of their music, literature and art.

But to return to the fortress; inside it there is a former garrison church where Peter and the Tsars after him lie buried. Under the belfry staircase lies Peter's son. So devoted was Peter to the task of modernizing Russia that when his son, an adherent of the old school, organized resistance to his father's plans, he had him executed and buried under the staircase of the belfry. He wanted to humiliate him even after death because people going up the tower would walk over his head.

But the most significant thing to me in that church was the fact that Peter's grave was the only one where wreaths and flowers had been placed. The people and the authorities in Russia today venerate the memory of Peter, and he was the only one in that church among the Tsars so venerated. Not even the Emperor Alexander II, the emancipator of the serfs, was so honoured.

Lenin has not unfittingly been called the twentieth-century Peter the Great. For, like Peter, he wanted to see a new Russia built up on councils of workers and peasants and not, as hitherto, by aristocrats, landlords and a few big business people. Like Peter, he was impressed with the backwardness of Russia and wanted to develop industry, which actually had begun even at the end of last century in Tsarist times, and thus he wanted to imitate the West. For Russia had not grown like Western Europe. Her whole development had been warped, thrown back and atrophied by the Mongol invasion. This prevented the influence of the Reformation from penetrating to her and she had remained in a mediaeval state of society till the end of the seventeenth century. Russia was still largely an Asiatic state with all the traditions of autocratic government accepted by the nomads of the Central Asian steppes for their protection. This caused Russia to become economically and socially behind the rest of Europe. Then Peter the Great forced her suddenly to make a great break with the past. He advanced the country economically and gave her an administration of some efficiency, but he did it by autocratic means, as was natural in a country of that tradition, and so the real state of the country, though improved in one way, was held back in another. For after Peter's death Russia stagnated again with short-lived periods of advance as under Alexander II. The next great chance to push Russia forward along the lines of Western European industrial and economic development came in the breakdown caused by the First World War. The economy of Russia was too weak to stand the strain and the fabric of the state collapsed in the war. Lenin seized his chance and gave Russia another push forward along the lines of the West. Having seen, therefore, where Peter worked, on the following day my wife and I went to see where, two and a half centuries later, Lenin worked. It was the Smolny Institute, the former school for the daughters of the aristocracy. Here the Leningrad Soviet used to meet and here I had been just over forty years ago and had been present at the birth of another new Russia.

It must not be forgotten, however, that right up to modern times there were people in Russia who thought that Peter the Great's innovations were a disaster for Russia. A whole school of thought grew up in the nineteenth century holding that Russia should *not* imitate the West but follow her own line, avoid the evils of industrialization and its accompanying poverty and slums and create a Slavonic way of life based on village communes and co-operative domestic industry. Such Russian politics as there were in the last half of the nineteenth century were largely concerned with this dichotomy. The Western school triumphed in the October Revolution and Lenin carried on the work that Peter the Great had begun. My wife and I went to see where he started his great work in those Autumn days of 1917 when the First World War was slowly grinding to a halt on the Eastern front.

When we visited the Smolny Institute, we found that official guides were there to take us round. I had last seen the building in the chaos that accompanied the October Revolution in 1917. In 1946, when I was last in Leningrad, the place had been closed. Now it is a show place. I looked at the clean and tidy entrance with its Doric columns and imagined I could see the companies of garrison troops and Red Guards jostling each other on their way in and out of the building. I remembered how I had to wait till one lot had passed and rush in before the next one came, in order to get to my destination. On the steps leading to the main entrance were now flower-pots where I remembered machine-guns being posted.

A guide took us into the great hall where the critical meetings of the All Russian Soviet Congress had been held, and where we waited hourly for news of what was happening on the revolutionary front. It was here that we heard of the capture of the Winter Palace by the two garrison regiments of Leningrad (Petrograd as it was then) and of the flight of Kerensky and of his Government. It was at that door which I looked at now that I had shown my pass as correspondent of the *Manchester Guardian*.

The guide gave us an official version of what took place, in tones that showed that he had learned it off by heart. There sat Lenin, there sat Sverdloff, he said. And 'What about Trotsky,' I asked. This caused hesitation for a moment. 'He was not there,' said the guide. 'Oh, yes he was,' I said, 'because I saw him there acting as chairman at least for the first few days.' The guide's face fell, and then I told him how I came to be there. He had not quite bargained for this. I embarrassed him still more when I added that I had nowhere seen Stalin till a fortnight after the seizure of power. Then I saw Sverdloff introduce him as Comrade Yugoshwili, the new Commissar of Nationalities, as if he was a hardly known person. Trotsky had meanwhile been appointed to a gigantic and vital task at Brest-Litovsk to arrange an armistice with the Germans. It was clear that there is still an official ban on any favourable mention of Trotsky, but at least it has now got to the point of just ignoring him, which is better than was once the case.

I found things different among the other attendants at the Smolny. One of them, who showed us the humble rooms where Lenin and his wife lived through those critical days, was clearly under no orders what to say, and when I told him that I had been there and what I had seen, he was immensely interested and got some of his colleagues to gather round us and plied me with questions about Lenin, Trotsky, Stalin and the others. I told them of Lenin's speech, which I had heard before we got the news of the fall of the Winter Palace and in which it seemed to me that he was a little uncertain and wavering in what to advise next. He had ended his speech with the very stereotyped phrase, 'Long Live the Revolutionary People', said in a tone without much enthusiasm. For Lenin was nothing if not a realist, and he always looked facts in the face. The attendants seemed fascinated with what I told them, and the fact that I was British did not seem to alter their judgment about what I had said. We then went to some other rooms where the Press Bureau once was and I remembered being given the various decrees issued by the Council of the People's Commissars, the revolutionary Government. Here indeed I saw the new Russia being created, even more thorough than the one created by Peter the Great, important as that was. For Peter, in spite of 'opening his window to the West' and laying the foundations of Russian industry and foreign trade, helped to rivet serfdom on the peasants and increased the power of the landlords whom he used to impress the peasants into his army. But Lenin finally broke the power of the landlords, as I saw when I read the decrees handed out by the Press Bureau years ago. In another place I had gone to see the offices of the Military Revolutionary Committee and, to my surprise, had met an American anarchist. It was a curious assortment of people who at that time had flocked to the Smolny Institute. It showed the international nature of the movement, but the internationalism was not of a very representative kind, for no one outside Russia seems to have known the American, Polish, Czech and Balkan people who, with the Russian revolutionaries, made up that Committee.

There is no doubt that Lenin was the driving force all through this critical moment in Russian history. If he had not been there, one can assume that the Revolution would have taken place, but in forms even more chaotic than what actually took place. He had an iron will and great ruthlessness but a great sense of realism. This iron will was absolutely essential in the condition of social and political dissolution existing in Russia at that time. But that was also a source of weakness when Lenin and his colleagues tried to inspire other countries on Russia's western borders, like Poland and Germany, to adopt a Communist system. Lenin's theory of government was that the Communist Party should be the source of power and should dominate the Soviets or councils of workers, soldiers and peasants. No other parties should be allowed and the 'dictatorship of the proletariat' was to become the dictatorship of the Party over the proletariat. This roused the opposition of a large section of the working classes of Central Europe who had been used to much greater freedom under their governments, and so their parties rejected the Russian methods. This split took place even in the Communist Party in Germany and the attitude of Rosa Luxembourg was typical of the opposition to Lenin's theory even on the Left Wing.[1] But those theories, while quite unsuitable for Central Europe, were historical necessities for Russia as she was at that time.

We went to one more memorial in Leningrad of the time when I was there forty and more years ago. That was the Taurida Palace. It was the residence once of an important personage in Tsarist days and now contains the offices and sessional hall of the Leningrad City

[1] See Chapter VIII, p. 94.

1   Timber Port at St Petersburg, 1908

Timber Port at Leningrad, 1959

2 Leningrad—Fortress of Peter and Paul and palaces on the Neva

Leningrad—
Smolny Institute and
statue of Lenin

Council. When I first knew it, it was the home of the Imperial Duma, the parliament of Russia which the Tsar had been forced to call as a result of the otherwise abortive revolution of 1905. That parliament was ignored by the Tsar's government, but it was a sounding-board for opinion and in that respect did good work. I saw it once in session in the First World War. But the most important thing I remembered about it was when it was the place where the Supreme Soviet met after it had left the Smolny Institute. After about a month at the latter place, it was found more convenient and had better premises. It looked rather different from what I remembered of it. There was the big hall, or central lobby, but the semicircular chamber with the rostrum and platform behind seemed to have been altered. But I saw what I thought was the press gallery where I spent one famous night. It was when the ultimatum from the German Generals arrived from Brest-Litovsk. It demanded cession of the Ukraine, the fertile corn belt of South-West Russia, the annexation of the Baltic provinces and many other humiliations. This was the first really serious crisis that the Revolutionary Government of Russia had had to face. The Revolution had succeeded beyond all hopes inside Russia. There was little real internal opposition except in the more outlying parts of the old Empire. But here were the jack-boots of a great foreign military power which was proposing to tear part of the vitals out of Russia. The Supreme Soviet Executive had been summoned together with the delegates of the All Russia Soviet Congress. I remembered talking to the delegates in the central lobby. 'Russia will be lost unless World Revolution breaks out in the rest of the world,' one delegate said to me, and that was the view of most of those present. That was the atmosphere prevailing at the time. The Russians were living in an ecstatic state of mind. They thought themselves the Messiahs of the world leading it to a new life. Just before the Revolution, the country had been sunk in gloom. We are dark, backward people, they used to say, and foreigners will come and rule us. When the Tsar and the weak Kerensky régime had gone, the flood-gates opened and an immeasurable hopefulness burst forth. The Russians were passing from the desire to complete the work of Peter the Great and imitate the West, to the desire to be modern Slavophils and show the people of the West that Russia had a better way of life. I heard the view expressed that night that Russia should defy the German Generals, withdraw her army (such as there was left of it) back to the Urals and cause the Germans to get bogged down in the vast spaces of Russia.

Then, while I was still in that gallery, I saw Lenin quietly come forward and address the great assembly. What is the use of words, he said. It is of no use to be 'slaves to phrases'. Only power matters, and that is what the German militarists understand and nothing else. We must gain a 'breathing-space' by accepting the terms and withdraw to husband our resources. The German militarists will have far to go to suppress us, even if they hold the Ukraine and the Baltic States. I remember the hush falling on the gallery and, as Lenin retired to his seat, I saw Madame Kollontai, a very prominent woman Communist, buttonhole him and call him a traitor to the Revolution. To cut a long story short, I sat there till about 2.0 in the morning, by which time a motion to accept the German terms was agreed by a majority with some abstentions. If the abstentions had voted against the motion, it would have been lost.

I had other memories of the Taurida Palace and I will relate them some day, but what I have described showed me quite early in the Revolution that, in spite of a sense of Messianic mission, there was an element of realism among some of the Russian Communist leaders. This was particularly the case with Lenin, and I began to realize then what I realized fuller later: how great a man he was. His advice in fact proved abundantly right. Nine months later, the German militarists were biting the dust. I have often wondered since what would have happened if, on that great night which I witnessed in the Taurida Palace, things had gone differently, and what course the Russian Revolution would then have taken. I cannot help feeling that this was one of the historic moments when personality *did* play a rôle in history or at least temporarily deflected it.

So on that day last autumn when I looked at the Taurida Palace I thought of what had happened just over forty years ago. How different the scene now was as the seat of the municipality of Leningrad. I saw clerks and typists moving out from their offices for lunch in the canteens across the way, and I doubt if any of them were aware of the tremendous events that had once happened in the place where they worked.

We saw something of the art and drama of Leningrad while we were there. The impression that I got was that it differed little from the old that I had always remembered. For instance, the classical plays and operas were as popular as ever and one saw little or no modern drama of the Soviet period. We witnessed 'Queen of Spades', that well-known work of two Russian giants of the past, Pushkin and Tschaikowsky, at the former Marinsky Theatre. The audience seemed highly to approve of the production. But English people whom we had met on the boat and who had also seen it were critical. They thought it was 'sentimental' and 'pretty-pretty', that the dances and songs did not always blend with one another and at times were out of place. Here I think is a failure to understand the reason for this aste of the Russian people. The Russian public looks forward to an opera or play as a great diversion from the dullness and drabness of their lives in the long winter nights both in city and provincial town. They want their enjoyments of song, dance and music concentrated and do not care if all the features fit in exactly with each other. The taste of the Russian public in this respect has changed little, because the nature of their lives in the physical conditions particularly of North Russia has not changed. What has changed is the fact that far more people can see music and drama now than ever before. But the desire for greater realism in the presentation of an opera like the 'Queen of Spades' is not there as it would be in Western Europe. This makes possible the English criticism that we heard. In any case, I think it is true that the West has now got its own way of presenting Russian works of musical art. I have seen a Covent Garden production of the 'Queen of Spades' in London, quite as good as, but somewhat different from, the productions in Russia. That used not to be the case, and I used to think that only Russian productions of their great classical works were worth seeing. One cannot think that now, for in many ways the Russians are more conservative and conventional. The Revolution, which established the Communist dictatorship over everything including art, has tended to make Russian art static and in some cases to force it into artificial channels. That is not true of the opera, because mercifully no one can improve upon the great classical Russian artists. The Communist régime, however, has prevented new interpretations.

In pictorial and plastic art, Leningrad has greatly developed even beyond the best time of the Tsars. More money has gone into the Hermitage, that unique collection of non-Russian painting and sculpture which now extends beyond its original building to include part of the neighbouring Winter Palace. This is now one of the world's greatest collections on a level with the Louvre. But there is now what I do not remember before, an important gallery of purely Russian painting and sculpture, the 'Russian Gallery'. Formerly the art collections of Leningrad gave the same impression as the city itself. It was deliberately non-Russian and in imitation of the West. Now one can see and compare West European and Oriental art side by side with Slavonic and Russian art if one visits the Hermitage and the 'Russian Gallery' together. It appears that one can see this better in Leningrad today than one can in Moscow, where the only great, and certainly supreme, art gallery is the Tretiakoff. Those who have planned the art of Leningrad have done a great work, and it is only within recent years that this has been done.

CHAPTER III

MOSCOW (Part I)

Intourist hotels and guides; memories of the past; visiting a Russian home; standards of living; Marxist economists; Russian economic unbalance; Russia's economic strength and weakness; building a new Moscow; technical and technological education; Russia's educational strength and weakness.

WE arrived in Moscow by the 'Golden Arrow' from Leningrad and before long were settled in the 'Ukraine', a well-appointed modern hotel, a minor skyscraper and right on the outskirts of the city. This seemed a rather serious impediment to doing things, because it would mean so much time lost in getting to the centre. Actually, Intourist's transport arrangements were so good that with reasonable notice we found that we could get cars to take us anywhere, wait for us or come and fetch us as required. Meals were often a trouble due to dilatory and incompetent waiters, but apologies for this were always forthcoming and there was more than one row and change of staff while we were there. Clearly these were teething troubles. The central hall of the 'Ukraine' was a big centre of movement. Travellers, both Russian and foreign, met their friends or the people they had to meet there. It was a great international gathering place and, since Russia is a vast country, one saw people from the outer parts of the Union, from Turkestan, Siberia and the Caucasus, who must have seemed foreigners to the average Muscovite.

We were very fortunate in our guide, a young lady student, who had just finished the University. She got on very well with my wife, and I found her intelligent and broad-minded and a great help to me. We discussed a lot of things together and I found that, though always standing up for her Russian point of view, she quite understood the view of foreigners, especially from Western Europe and America. Irma was the kind of guide whom Intourist should try and get more of. She and those like her would do more to raise Russia's stock abroad than all the sputniks in the world. It is interesting that Russian universities seem to be turning out young people of this kind. It must be all part of the thaw since the passing of Stalin.

During the time we were in Moscow, I succeeded through Intourist, through the Russian division of the Inter-Parliamentary Union and through my own personal and timber business contacts, in meeting quite a number of informative people. They were in the field of politics, politico-economic science, pure science, education (both humanities, technical and technological), industry and local government (particularly housing). My wife, while attending some of these meetings, went off with Irma to explore the shops, State and co-operative stores and social welfare. I found it not so easy to get down to the people as in Leningrad, because, as I said before, Moscow is the capital and everybody is very busy. But here and there one saw down into the way the Muscovites live through the bustle and stir of life above.

Before I attempt to describe my impressions, I will give three pictures of what I remember of Moscow in former times, fifty, forty-five and forty-two years ago, in comparison with today. Before the First World War in 1910 I was visiting Russia for a short while with two colleagues, starting off on a scientific expedition across south-west Siberia and Outer Mongolia. I went in Moscow to see some Russian scientists and professional people who would help me with work I was then doing for this expedition. After getting the information that I required, we talked over a samovar about the future of Russia. They were full of gloom. The old régime was killing Russia, they said; the people were 'dark' and the régime deliberately kept them so. Russia would fall a prey to the people of the West. That would mean Germany, and they feared for Russia. A few years later, during the First World War, I heard the same thing from the 'dark' people themselves, not in Moscow but from peasants at a railway station waiting for a train in the Ukraine. 'Russia is dark,' they said, 'the English, French and Germans will come and rule us as the Varangs did of old.' That was fifty years ago. Forty-five years ago in 1915 I came to Moscow again and saw some merchants in the timber business in the Kitai Gorod, the commercial centre of the old city. There was a change now, the war with Germany was on and everyone was patriotic. They were convinced they would win the war with the help of France and England and then a new Russia would arise. Outside in the street I saw plundered German shops and the debris left by police-led mobs and I wondered what this 'new Russia' really was going to be. Forty-two years ago in 1918 I had been in this same Moscow again after the October Revolution and after the transfer of the capital from Petrograd. In what is now the National Hotel in the square outside the Kremlin, I attended during the spring and summer of 1918 the meetings of the All Russia Soviet Executive. The Bolshevik or Communist revolutionaries were in a state of great exultation. Russia had defied the world and had shown it a new way of life. But the rest of the world must follow or Russia would perish, said many of the delegates of the Soviet Executive to me. 'Was it necessary,' I said to them, 'that all the world should become Communist for Russia to be saved?' Opinion forty-two years ago amongst the revolutionary leaders in Moscow said yes.

Today, I found a different atmosphere again. The firm attitude of America and the West and the fact that the rest of Europe had gone its own way in finding solutions of the social and economic problems after two world wars had caused Russian Communists to re-think their philosophy once more. In a large house in the very part of the city where once I had spoken to the Soviet delegates in 1918, I found the able and broad-minded leaders of the Institute for World Economy and International Relations. They were all Communists, but they had realized that Communism would spread throughout the world by example alone. The pace could not be forced. They had not changed their aims, but they had changed their tactics. I will return to this theme later and show the way their minds seem to be working today.

From what one learns from talking to people in the streets and shops and from the prices one sees in the stores, the impression one gets in Moscow is the same as in Leningrad; that the incomes of the people are comparatively good even by Western standards, but that they are much more heavily eroded than in the West by the prices of durable and non-durable consumer goods. Particularly did my wife and I get this impression when we visited one of the new housing estates on the southern outskirts of Moscow. At the Municipal Housing Centre we asked if we could see inside a typical flat, and this request was granted. We were taken to the flat of a Soviet professional man, an architect and his wife living in two rooms and a son and his wife, he an engineer and she a teacher, living in the third room. Two full incomes of over 1,000 roubles a month were going in and a third, the father's, was supplemented by a pension, for owing to war-time injuries he could not earn a full income. Still, an equivalent of 2,500 roubles a month was probably going into that three-roomed flat which, at the tourist rate of exchange, would be about £20 a week.

Yet one could not help observing the relative poverty of equipment in the house. We saw no refrigerators or washing machines, no electric cookers or ironers. Hoovers, in any case, one never sees except in hotels and big institutions. The equipment was no better than a working-class family would have had in the nineteen-twenties in Western Europe. There was, however, a small wireless set, which, as I mentioned above, are relatively cheap in Russia. But colour and taste were absent. A pathetic bunch of half-dead flowers drooped in a vase on the table. Furniture was of the simplest kind. But then nowhere in Russia did we see furniture stores with the wide range of choice to be seen in Western Europe. The simple furniture that one does see must come from some of the co-operative or State stores, but their simplicity indicates why they are not exhibited in showrooms, because the choice is so small. They are bought apparently in lots when one sets up house. The only conclusion that one could come to was that the average Russian professional man and civil servant, other than those of the higher grades, find that the prices are too high, and that makes them keep their demands down to the minimum. They prefer to spend money on books, the opera and theatre, all of which are very cheap, cheaper in fact than in the West. For the Soviet State and the municipalities provide many things on a non-economic basis for the benefit of the citizen. Books particularly are cheap, and in the flat that we visited both in the rooms of the old and the young generation were shelves full of books. Here we saw no Marxist classics, no full works of Lenin and Stalin, but Victor Hugo, Balzak, Galsworthy, Dickens and Shakespeare. When I told them that the England of Dickens was not the England of today, they well understood and expressed a strong desire to visit England and see how her people lived there.

I am certain the flat that we saw was typical of the great majority of Soviet citizens living in the cities and towns. But, of course, there has developed in recent years a small tier in Russian society, enjoying a higher standard of living than the average. The national income is more equally distributed now than it has ever been, but new levels in society are developing. I remember controversies in the early days of the October Revolution about how egalitarian a society should be. Lenin and the majority of the leaders saw that they could not get expert talent to serve the Soviet State without paying for it. The more dogmatic of their followers, however, thought this terrible and that it would bring back the evils of capitalist society again. Lenin and his friends, however, got their way and now one has a technically very important, though not numerous, class of Soviet citizens with higher incomes than the rest, with private cars, good flats and bungalows for the summer. They are the higher bureaucrats, the technocrats, the top industrial executives and the leading artists, actors and ballet dancers. As there is virtually no income tax, it is possible for this class even to start accumulating capital by investing in State loans and handing on to their children. These are the people referred to in that famous book *Not By Bread Alone* by Duditseff. Mr Krushchev sees the danger of this development, and his popularity, which is great, is derived in part from the fact that he is known to favour policies which will bring the higher standard of living enjoyed by this relatively narrow circle of society down to the much wider circle of the lower professional and working classes.

One of the most informative talks I had in Moscow on the development of the Russian economy and on the philosophy of its Communist leaders was with one of the heads of the Institute of World Economy and International Relations, corresponding to Chatham House in London. Some of their top men like M. Solodovnikoff are examples of the new type of Communist thinkers. I found them frank and broad-minded. They admit that it is State policy to concentrate on capital goods, scientific development and heavy industry and thus to hold back the production of consumer goods for a time. The danger seems to be that the gap between scientific achievements and the general standard of living of the people is widening. The former is racing ahead, the latter is stationary. But as was pointed out to me at the Institute, much relief would come from general disarmament and I found this a constant theme not only in these quarters but with the man in the street. I even noticed a fear that some accident might spark off a war.

The actual number of Communists organized in the Party is not more than about three per cent. of the population but they are the driving force and a source of authority. The Institute of World Economy and International Relations undoubtedly have considerable say in Government policy and I found their general view about the future of Communism very interesting. Gone are the days which I remember during the Revolution when Communism had to spread like wildfire throughout the world by any means that could be found. It has clearly come to the minds of the top men in the Communist Party in Russia that Western Europe and America have found another way. I found that the emphasis now was on the spread of Communism in the undeveloped areas of Asia and Africa. It would be here that Communism and private enterprise would compete and the system which is the most successful in helping the people of these countries would ultimately be accepted by them. I found the people at the Institute pointing out to me that Russian Communism has a great advantage here. They showed me figures which they had collected showing how Britain had invested overseas over the last half of the nineteenth century large capital sums, but had drawn out from these countries in Asia and Africa in food, raw material and profits much more than she had put in. The same was true of France, and they showed me figures of this too. If they were correct figures or not, I could not say, so for the time being I accepted them, but pointed out that, even if it had been true, as it very well might have been, it was not true now, that these countries were awakening, that Britain had seen this in advance and was offering independence to these countries as they gradually were able to take over the reins of government themselves. Moreover, this was not just in the future, but had actually happened in Asia and was in process of happening in Africa. 'Therefore,' I said, 'although you may have an initial advantage, I think we are now on a level with you and we are taking out from these countries no more than fair interest on capital investments. Indeed, the United States has been extremely generous and given enormous sums to these countries with no thought of return. Our resources are not so great, but we have done something on these lines too.' I found they admitted all that I was saying, and the discussion was of a most objective and friendly nature. They pointed out to me that Russia was now offering loans at two and a half per cent., to be repaid over ten years, for public works in India, Egypt and the Middle East. From other sources I heard later that their contract prices for public works in these countries compare quite favourably with those of the West. One of the Institute leaders put it to me that much depends on how soon these capital investments will have effect on the lives of the people. The latter are in a hurry, and have been led by wireless propaganda to expect better conditions of living soon. So the contest is certainly on between the Communist and the 'Free Economy' systems in those parts of the world.

What I saw in the architect's house and what I heard from the able political-economists at the Institute of World Economy and International Relations caused me to reflect not only on the competition which is now on between Russia and the West in the undeveloped areas of Asia and Africa, but also on the internal state of Russia today and how she is able to finance this great effort abroad. The October Revolution which I had witnessed forty and more years ago was the explosion which swept away a form of Russian society which was hindering economic and social advance. The Civil War which followed for a time stopped every advance, but since the last war there has been nothing to prevent progress on all fronts.

But when one looks at the internal situation in Russia and tries to interpret it, one can only come to the conclusion that Russia is still in the primitive non-durable consumer goods and early capital construction stage. By the latter, I mean that she is still opening out new minefields, building steel plants, founding new industries and doing on a big scale what most of Western Europe and America have already done or are in process of finishing. But she has hardly begun her road development which elsewhere, of course, is in full swing. Instead of finishing this and getting well into the non-durable consumer goods stage and providing her people with their full requirements of clothing, footwear and simple household goods which are relatively cheap in price, she is forcing herself into the advanced stage of capital goods construction. Not only is she still opening out minefields, building railways and constructing steel plants, but she is far advanced in jet propulsion, aircraft, machine tools and the exploration of outer space. This is an altogether artificial set-up and results in Russia being in some forms of industrial production ahead of all other countries in the world, yet behind in matters of ordinary clothing and footwear for the civil population, where supplies are inferior in quality, scarce in quantity and dear in relation to wages when compared with Western Europe and America. There is here, of course, a question of prestige. The world talks about Russia and is greatly impressed by her scientific discoveries and their application to industry. It is easy to get the impression from this that Russia is surpassing Western Europe and America as the dominant industrial power of the world. It is true, of course, that Russia may soon be able to export planes and machine tools at less than the cost that the rest of the world can produce them at. She may in consequence attract to herself the undeveloped states of Asia and Africa who are only just getting into the non-durable consumer goods stage and have not yet begun the early capital goods production stage. She may become the power that can successfully equip them in the shortest time and thus enable them to pass quickly into the non-durable consumer goods stage. This may or may not affect the political systems of these undeveloped countries of Asia and Africa. But, in any case, Russia can only do this by keeping her own people down to a level only one stage above these countries of Asia and Africa. She is keeping herself artificially in the early non-durable consumer goods stage and delaying the period of passing into the durable consumer goods stage. For instance, she has not begun the stage which Western Europe and America have been in for some time of producing such goods as cheap motor cars for the masses, refrigerators and all the hundred and one articles of household equipment which housewives in the West have had for a long time. I have little doubt from what I saw in Russia that this is the price they are paying for their tremendous development in jet propulsion, sputniks and their drive to develop the countries of Asia and Africa. It is the sort of thing that can be done in a Communist country where a small intellectual aristocracy rules and has not, as in the democratic countries of the West, to consider public opinion so much. On the other hand, the impression I got was that they are not indifferent altogether to public opinion and this is Mr Krushchev's strength. This is not the first time that there has been an unbalance in the economy of Russia. I remember the time before the Revolution when Russia exported much corn to the world markets and was an important factor on these markets. Yet she only did this by starving her peasants and exporting corn which should have gone into their mouths.

In this respect also it seems that this is a matter of internal politics. A rapid rise in the standard of living of the Russian masses might lead to awkward consequences for the Communist Party. As I said above, the Communist Government is not subject to such pressure from its own public opinion that it has immediately to do what is wanted. It is obvious that if the durable consumer goods stage is reached soon, the average Soviet citizen will begin to want and to get private motor cars and week-end bungalows in the country and altogether to be more independent and less under control. And after all it is easier for the police to see who are living in a block of flats and who visits them than if the inmates can go at any time by car to a bungalow on the edge of the forest some fifty miles away from town.

Yet Mr Krushchev knows quite well that this sort of change is coming and that not even a Communist Government can resist it, even if it wants to. Mr Krushchev seems to fancy himself in the rôle of the popular liberator after the strait-jacket of the Stalin era, just as Alexander II fancied himself as the Tsar-Liberator after the harsh winter of discontent under his father. But Mr Krushchev seems to be making haste slowly. He certainly wants a gradual improvement in the standard of living of the people, but not a flood which may let loose forces difficult to control. The Communist Party even in Poland, where relaxation has gone much further, retains the right to have the last word in every situation. The Communist leaders, including Mr Krushchev, have no intention of allowing this to be altered. And public opinion is likely to be satisfied if it sees a gradual approach to a more plentiful and cheaper consumer goods stage than exists at present. The indications are there that Russia is as interested in peace and the raising of living standards as we in the West. Everything points to a process of cooling going on and to a desire to spread Communism by example instead of the more aggressive form.

Public opinion in Western Europe is interested to know just how successful the Russians are going to be in capturing the markets of the world and especially the undeveloped areas of Asia and Africa. In the Labour Party there is a body of opinion that takes it almost as a foregone conclusion that because in Russia the economy is planned and State-owned, therefore the Russians will automatically be in a position industrially to forge ahead of the West. Without doubt an economy which makes the motives of private profit an important influence on production and the securing of markets has a more difficult task than one which is State-owned and planned and where directions from above can canalize activity as required. The Russian Communists have, as I show above, by Government action at the top deliberately deprived their people of consumer goods, household equipment, the people's car, etc., all of which exist in abundance in the West. Instead, they have concentrated on such things as the Assuan Dam for the Egyptians, steel mills for Indians, armaments and the exploration of outer space with sputniks. We, on the other hand, have preferred to liberalize our economy, remove Government controls and allow private industry to provide in competition all the consumer goods that the people can buy with hire-purchase credits and bank advances. The result is that the goods are produced and produced cheaply, but there is a constant danger of inflation, overstraining the home consumers' market, while exports tend to sag and private business finds it easier to make profits at home than to do so by competing with Russian State-controlled industry in Asia and Africa. There is no doubt that this is the weak spot in the economy of the West and especially of Britain, and the Communist countries do possess certain advantages in this respect.

And yet one is entitled to doubt if an economy like that of Russia is all that efficient in the long run compared with the West. One has only to read the Soviet press to realize that from time to time, and not all that infrequently either, writers and journalists on behalf of the public complain of bureaucratic inefficiency and long delays in coming to decisions over vital matters affecting the economy. Actually I heard these complaints in connection with the timber trade, in which I am interested. It was very hard to know in advance just how much timber Russia will export each year and how much she will put on her home market, until the last minute when decisions must be made. At times there are definite breakdowns in the working of the industrial machine and, to do the Communists justice, they are not hushed up but spoken of openly with a view to remedy. Russia is a vast country, and although in the modern world distances are growing less, they are still great in the area between the Baltic and the Pacific Ocean, and the Russian people over parts of this enormous expanse of territory are still uninfluenced by the ideas of efficiency and speed. Life is still very easy over large areas. The bureaucratic machine has been called into existence in the past because of Russia's size and backwardness. This problem has not yet been solved and, when coupled with the fact that Russia has only advanced to the point that she has in science, technology and industry by deliberately holding back the standard of living of her people, it will be seen that she has a long way to go yet before she can be up to the general level of prosperity and efficiency of the West, let alone surpass it. There is no evidence that Russia is automatically overhauling the West, nor is there any likelihood of this happening if the West tempers its private enterprise economy with a certain degree of planning and central direction without creating a vast State machine which tends to clog the wheels.

I kept on seeing places in Moscow where I remembered important things happening forty and more years ago and where I heard significant speeches. For instance, in one street on the edge of the Kitai-Gorod I heard Lenin after the Brest-Litovsk Peace, when Soviet Russia was humiliated and valuable parts had been torn away, make a great speech which was later published under the title *The Next Problem before the Soviet Power*. It was a remarkable speech, because here Lenin told his followers bluntly that they must learn from the capitalist states how to run a government and a country and cease to be 'academic phrase-mongers'. When one looks at Russian scientific and industrial achievements today, one realizes how well Lenin's lesson has been learned, though as I show above, Russian economy is unbalanced, progress having been made very much on one side and very little on another.

In another place near the Arbat I found a place where I remembered hearing Trotsky, returning from the front during the Civil War with the Russian Whites, aided by foreign interventionists, give a factual account of the state of the campaign and rouse the audience to great enthusiasm. In this respect all my impressions of Trotsky were that he was, next to Lenin, the most powerful and effective of the revolutionary leaders during a crisis. He was the Danton of the Revolution and, like Danton, he laid the seeds of his own undoing. I noticed even then in his speeches the domination of the idea of World Revolution, as if Communism must come throughout the world if Russia was to be saved. The idea that the Socialist Soviet system could survive in Russia and not spread throughout the world did not seem to enter his mind. His theory was known as the 'Permanent Revolution' which must always be moving on and affecting other countries after it had started in Russia.

I had left Russia before the great rivalry started between Trotsky and Stalin. The latter I never saw at all during the summer of 1918 in Moscow. Only later did he come into great prominence as secretary to the Political Bureau of the Russian Communist Party. It was he who started the idea of 'Socialism in One Country' which did much to undermine Trotsky's influence. Since the World Revolution did not break out either in Germany or Italy, the two countries in Central Europe which seemed ready for revolution, the Russian idea was rejected after 1918. Thus Stalin was shown to be the greater realist.

Stalin's policy was to leave the rest of the world alone, not to force the pace, make use of revolutions if they broke out elsewhere but withdraw from supporting them if they proved a failure or too costly, as in Spain. Meanwhile Russia should concentrate on building up her defences and become the 'Socialist Soviet Motherland' and create as far as possible a chain of satellite states on Russia's western borders for her defence. This, in fact, is what happened, and Stalin showed himself more practical in these matters than Trotsky and more in touch with the world situation. Still, Trotsky was the more picturesque and heroic character, while Stalin in his later life developed the evil qualities of a tyrant. The danger of government by oligarchy, which is the Soviet system, is that power may get into one man's hand and he become a megalomaniac. It happened with Napoleon after the French Revolution and it happened with Stalin after the Russian Revolution. But we cannot gainsay the fact that initially Stalin's foreign policy for Russia was right. All these impressions came back to me as I looked at the places where I had seen great events and heard great speeches and as I reflected on how history had marched on since those days forty and more years ago.

Another memory of the past came to me when I went to the 'Bolshoi' Opera House to see a performance of 'Swan Lake'. It was here where, in July 1918, I had been shut up for about twelve hours during a session which I attended of the All-Russia Soviet Congress. A revolt against the Communists had broken out and fighting was going on in the streets outside, while all delegates to the Congress were shut in till it was over and one side or the other had won. We sat there hour after hour and only managed to get a cup of tea and some dry bread. At about half-time there was a violent explosion in the upper gallery. Someone had placed a time bomb there. Sverdloff, who was chairman of the Congress, kept his head and calmed everyone and finally we were told the cause of all this.

When the Communists had taken power in October 1917, there were other parties who supported their action. But they were not Marxists, i.e. they did not hold the theories of so-called 'economic determinism' which the Communists held. They did not believe in an urban working-class dictatorship. They did not believe in Russia passing through an industrial stage at all, but were advocates of the so-called 'revolutionary peasants', who would seize the land from the landlords and set up rural communes to work the land in common. In this way, it was thought that Russia would avoid the evil effects of industrialization which had taken place in Western Europe and America. They were also believers in individual terror and assassination and had broken with the Communists over the Peace Treaty with the Germans. They wanted to carry on a revolutionary war with Germany and after the Brest-Litovsk Treaty they had left the coalition government, which they had entered on the first days of the October Revolution. Unknown to us that morning, they had murdered the German Ambassador in his Embassy, had seized two railway stations, the central telegraph office and had surrounded the Kremlin, where some of the Moscow garrison was. The Soviet Congress had been called for that day, and if the revolt had succeeded, the Congress would have been faced with an accomplished fact that the Communists had been overthrown and a 'real' revolutionary government of the Left wing of the Socialist Revolutionary Party and of the Anarchists had taken over power in Russia. However, it did not happen like that, and after a few hours' fighting the Communists were able to re-establish the position, the insurgents were disarmed and their leaders imprisoned. Early in the morning of the following day, we were let out of the 'Bolshoi' Opera House and Moscow was normal again. The whole affair was a culmination of the process by which the dominant Communist and Marxist revolutionaries were ridding themselves of elements which had played for years a great part in Russian revolutionary history but were now becoming out of date. They had at times dominated the movement. It was they who assassinated the Emperor Alexander II and who had led the peasant revolts in the revolution of 1905. But they were impractical people and the Communists always found them difficult to work with. This was then the revolt of the extreme Left against the revolutionary Centre. I witnessed it that day in July 1918, and it all came back that evening as I attended the ballet and saw the place where I had sat under very different circumstances and where the bomb had exploded forty-one years ago.

The enormous progress that Russia has made in the reconstruction of the country, the rebuilding of cities and towns, the building of factories, public works, canals and railways (but not yet roads) causes one to wonder how the technical skill has been created for this purpose. The results strike one at every turn. For instance, I scarcely recognized Moscow. It was a completely different place to the Moscow I had once known. One can recognize the streets around the Kremlin and along the Moscow river, one can see the Arbat much as it once was, and here and there are some of the old wooden houses that one associates with the Moscow that resisted Napoleon in 1812. I lived in one of them in the summer of 1918 when I stayed with Sergei Tolstoy and his wife, the eldest son of the great Leo Tolstoy. The house was still there, but large areas all round are completely reconstructed with a mushroom growth of small skyscrapers, and even what formerly were open fields are now built-up areas. The old city used to end at the Novo-Divichi monastery with its little Kremlin wall, one of the many walled monasteries that used to surround Moscow in mediaeval times. I used to wander from it down to the River Moscow across open fields to a spot opposite the Swallow Hills where Napoleon first looked on the domes of the Kremlin. Now a great stadium is erected by the river and houses and streets are all around. Farther up the river, at a place called Fili, there used to be a little church built in memory of the deliverance from Napoleon. I used often to walk there in the cool of a summer evening in 1918. The church is still there, but is overshadowed now by a factory with endless streets and buildings. Not far away from the church there was a little wooden hut where General Kutusov, the Russian commander-in-chief, decided in 1812 with his generals to evacuate Moscow. The little hut is now a museum. The Swallow Hills not far away are now called the Lenin Hills, and in the course of the last ten years the new buildings of Moscow University have been erected there. It is a most imposing building and shows a certain originality in style. In this immense building are in process of being housed the scientific laboratories for original research for which Russia is becoming so famous. But when I looked back on the Russia that I once knew, I remembered that in those days too Russia was turning out great scientists such as Menshikoff, Pavloff and others. But under the Soviet régime more talents get to the top and quicker and are not suppressed as much as they were formerly. The Russians are an able and talented people and their long winter nights give them time to be good mathematicians. Hence their progress in the physical sciences. But the question arises, are they turning out as good quality scientists, technicians and engineers as they used to? Or is the education turning out immense numbers of average scientists, with no great increase at the top level? I had no means frankly of gauging this while I was in Moscow, but I could say that the education system can and does turn out a very large and increasing number of technicians and technologists of moderate ability with a certain number of absolutely top people, probably more than before.

On this question I was able to get some first-hand impressions. For instance, I visited the Technical Institute, Ostinkino. This Institute trains pupils from the secondary schools to become skilled artisans and technicians, but not first-grade engineers and technologists for which a higher qualification is needed. I found that two streams of recruits are taken from the secondary schools, one which reaches grade seven in four years and the other which reaches grade twelve in two and a half years. Having completed part of their courses at what corresponds to our grammar or secondary modern schools, these pupils are allowed to specialize so as to become eventually skilled workers in factories. It seems that their general

3   Moscow—Cathedral of the Assumption in the Kremlin

Moscow—Kremlin gardens with Mrs Price and guide in foreground
and Church of Vassily Blazhenye in background

Moscow—modern Russian architecture, the new university

Kieff—public park on hills

education ceases when they enter the Technical Institute and that from then on full specialization is allowed. If there is any more general education such as history or literature, it is voluntary and takes the form of evening classes connected with the university. Half the technical training is theoretical and done through lectures, and the other half is practical demonstrations in laboratories and workshop courses. It seemed that about half the pupils were women who proposed to enter factories as skilled workers. About ten per cent. of the population were from Asiatic countries, China, Indonesia and Vietnam. Here one sees what Russia is doing in helping to open up and educate undeveloped countries. Enquiries that I made elicited the fact that the teachers and instructors at this Institute were much impressed by the pupils from Vietnam, whose work they found was 'surprisingly accurate considering their age'. There were many pupils also from Russian Central Asia, such as Usbeks, Tadjiks and Turcomans. The work of these pupils, I was told, was 'Not at all bad'.

On another occasion I visited the Bauman Institute, which corresponds to one of our technological colleges, either connected with a university or on its own. This place turns out people who will go on to pure science research or become higher engineers, chemists, electricians and persons who will be engaged in planning big public works and the application of scientific discoveries to industries. This form of applied science has made enormous strides in Russia and about one hundred thousand pupils, who have been through this course, are turned out annually in Russia today. The Bauman Institute is turning out about one thousand five hundred a year, engineers, chemists and electricians, getting, to start off with, a thousand roubles a month and rising to much higher figures later according to the jobs they succeed in getting.

The Institute takes pupils from the secondary schools at sixteen and gives them four- to five-year courses with intense specialization as from that age. The first year's work is in a factory with evening classes. The later years are mainly intensive theoretical training with lecture courses. One has the impression that these courses and the teaching generally is in no way inferior to anything in our technical colleges. This seems to indicate that, with the exception of the United States, no other country in the world is turning out the same number of technologists proportionately to the population. It is here where Russia has made astonishing strides in recent years. But these facts and figures need not make one think that Russia is necessarily outstripping the West. Numbers are not everything, and Russia is herself an undeveloped country requiring a very large number of engineers and technical people who are not of the first rank for the

D

development of public works of all kinds which the country still requires. No country in Europe has need to put such public schemes in operation as the Volga-Don canal, the irrigation schemes in Central Asia and the opening up of the Kazak steppes. The number of people required for these enormous works is much greater than would be required in Western Europe. All this is quite apart from the higher nuclear power schemes and inter-space research which require first-class people. Of course, all this is putting Russia in a position to compete well in the public works schemes in Asia and Africa which are coming along, like the Assuan Dam. On the other hand, there is always the question of quality in this type of education, and here I noticed something which seemed to indicate a deficiency in the Russian training.

The Bauman Institute has no contact with the universities. There is nothing to broaden the pupil's mind or to make him see the subject that he is studying in relation to the other activities of mankind. One foreign language is compulsory and sixty per cent. take English, twenty per cent. French and twenty per cent. German. History and economics are only taught as part of the instruction on Communist lines and are not compulsory. There are, of course, books that can be borrowed on the theory of Marxism and Communism, and there is a general teaching of Marxist theories. The technical education is narrow. Students learn only one process by a few machines and not the process as a whole or in relation to other processes. The training, however, is very good and the machines as good as anything in this country. The higher technical courses are for five years after eleven years of general education are completed. The impression one gets is that the pupils come out of the Institute as very efficient technologists but with little knowledge of history or of the world around them. Russian higher technical education turns out the specialists and the quantities, but one has reason to be sceptical about the outlook and quality of the young people. Of course, individuals of genius are picked out and pushed on to pure research and top jobs. Since the Revolution, more people are taking these courses than under the old régime and consequently there are more first-class people than there used to be. But one may be doubtful about the quality of large numbers who come out of these technological institutes in Russia today because the general training tends to be narrow.[1]

I got some figures which seemed to indicate the great specialization which has taken place in Russia in science and technology. It seems reasonable to compare in this respect Russia with the United States.

[1] In January 1960, after my visit to Russia, Mr Krushchev instituted an educational reform which aims to somewhat broaden the curriculum of education generally in Russia.

Both countries are continents with a very large population, the Russian being the largest. In 1959 the graduates of colleges and universities in all fields of study, both in science and technology on the one hand and in the humanities on the other, were a little over four and a half million in the United States and three and a quarter million in the Soviet Union. On the other hand, those working in the scientific and technical fields were just under one and a half million in the United States and one and three quarter million in the Soviet Union. This supports my impression that Russia is specializing greatly in science and technology and is giving the humanities second place; which is not the case in the United States. The educational drive on all fronts seems to be greater in the Soviet Union, for the annual rate of increase of those studying in all fields is seven per cent. in the Soviet Union and three and a half per cent. in the United States. Further confirmation that this drive is going in a certain direction can be seen from the number of graduates for higher degrees in 1958. It was ninety thousand for engineering and seventy thousand for general science in Russia, thirty-seven thousand for engineering and sixty-five thousand for general science in the United States. But even if it is recognized that Russia will probably continue her lead over the West and even increase it in the number of scientists and technologists that she turns out in proportion to her population, I think that the West is on sounder ground in its general education policy and in mingling the arts with the sciences. This is the only sound policy if one aims at turning out good men and not only efficient human machines.

CHAPTER IV

MOSCOW (Part II)

Municipal housing; a visit to a factory; a visit to the university; meeting students; talks with professors; the agricultural exhibition and glimpses of Central Asia; the Timber Export Trust; disappointment over Vladimir; a special visit to the Kremlin; the theatre and the Tretiakoff Art Gallery; the memory and influence of Lenin.

ONE of the weak spots of the Russian economy has undoubtedly been the serious lag in the provision of houses for the people. The enormous drive for technical education, scientific research and armaments has not only held back the production of consumer goods, both durable and non-durable, as I have described above, but has practically held up the building of houses until recently. Particularly bad in this respect has been the capital, Moscow, where the concentration of population engaged on Government work of all kinds has brought about a well-nigh catastrophic situation. It is not so bad in the provincial towns, though quite bad enough, but, as I show in the chapter on Leningrad, there were parts of this old city where houses are empty and going derelict.

My wife and I asked to see what the municipal authorities are doing in Moscow where the problem is worst, and we were afforded every facility to investigate. We were taken to one of the municipal housing centres to the south of the Moscow river. Here, in an area of several miles square, are acres and acres of new blocks of flats extending almost as far as the eyes can see. The areas are divided into groups of flats and each group has an administrative centre. We were told that the housing drive started in the spring of 1958 and that between then and the autumn of 1959 one hundred thousand families had been re-housed. Taking an average of five to the family, that would mean about half a million people have been given new homes. That would also mean that there are one hundred thousand new flats, but the figures they gave us were for less, so obviously more than one family in many cases still live in one flat. That also proved to be the case in the flat which we visited, where two families, a husband and wife and a son and daughter-in-law, were living in one flat. That also corresponded with what we were told, namely, that the standard flat consists of three rooms for four adult persons. That may seem little for our standards, but one has to bear in mind that housing standards in Russia have never been high. I remember in Tsarist times living with a family in Tiflis for several months in which there were seven persons in three rooms and I had one of those three, a single small room to myself, so that there were six living in two rooms. It seems that there is a better ratio today if, on an average, four or five live in three rooms. Looking out from the municipal housing centre, which we were visiting, across the sea of flats, one could get the impression that the figures which we were given and which we worked out for ourselves might very well be correct.

The standard rent for three rooms is sixty roubles a month, which at the tourist rate of exchange would be about £2, or 10s. a week. That certainly could not be called dear, and the municipality must subsidize houses to a considerable extent, although we did not find out how much. In fact, I do not think that anyone in the housing centre knew. We found a number of people from municipalities from all over Russia visiting this centre at the same time as us. One from as far away as Tiflis in the Caucasus we met later in Kieff. They all had come to see what was being done in Moscow and then went on to the other towns before returning to make plans to solve their own housing problems. We found that a certain number of flats were four-roomed and for these the rent was more than sixty roubles a month. There are, of course, extra charges for lighting, heating and telephone. It was central heating based on coal, and it did not seem that there was any electric heating at all. In general, one got the impression that the standard of housing is lower than in Western Europe but better than it used to be in Russia before the Revolution and better than in the satellites like Poland. All this tends to confirm the impression that Russia, so advanced in some aspects of science, is behind the West of Europe not only in articles of common consumption but also in housing.

I had heard a good deal about Mr Krushchev's programme for de-centralizing industry and curbing the enormous influence of the top-heavy bureaucracy in Russia. So I asked to see a factory, not one of the big show factories which visitors are generally taken to, but an average, small and not necessarily very up-to-date factory of which I knew there were a lot about. It was in due course arranged and my wife and I were taken one morning to a medium-sized factory employing about six hundred people and making curtains and printed covers for furniture. The factory building was not at all new, having been built towards the end of last century. But it had been adapted and enlarged. Some of the machinery was quite old, but some new looms had been bought from the East German Republic. Certainly the quality of the articles produced was excellent, and plenty of scope was offered for artistic talent to show itself. A number of artists were busy producing designs of scenes from Russian fairy-stories of an altogether delightful kind. The management were good enough to present my wife with a wall-hanging with a design illustrating one of these stories. On our return home we gave it to our grandchild.

The factory, we found, came under the general administration of the Sovnarhoz, the big Department of State which controls a number of industries. The Sovnarhoz appoints the management and leaves the industry to run itself in matters of detail. The management does not apparently now have to refer everything to the top when they want to scrap an old machine and get a new one. The control is more indirect and operates through the inspection of the finances and balance sheets at the end of the year. Also control is exercised over the sale prices which can be charged for the finished products. This is arranged in negotiation between the Sovnarhoz and the Government Department of Internal Trade on the one hand and the management of the factory on the other. Apparently now these State Departments are regionalized. In the case of this factory, the region was Moscow and an area round it. This Committee has power to fix sale prices for that area which need not necessarily be the same for all areas in the country. Thus there is a good deal more local industrial autonomy than there used to be. Production costs and wages now vary according to the regions, and sale prices vary too. There is obviously less strait-jacketing of industry than there used to be. If any part of the factory's finished product is sold abroad, the Department of Foreign Trade has to be consulted. Here greater uniformity is insisted upon, but as far as home trade is concerned, the law of supply and demand and free prices is beginning to appear again. Of course, it is always possible to tighten up controls if things get out of hand. But for the moment the trend is the other way. I asked if there had been any market hold-ups as regards curtains and furniture covers, because I had heard that in some products for domestic consumption factories had over-produced, yet the products had not got on the market through bureaucratic log-jams. The management admitted that there had been a few years ago something like this, but not for some time now.

As regards the wages and conditions of the workers, we found that all of them belonged to the Moscow Regional Union of the Textile Workers. Here again there has been greater de-centralization. Thus union and factory management negotiate an agreement on wages and conditions and this has not got to be approved by an All-Russia organization at the top, although the agreement has to be registered with them. These local agreements are now on a regional basis. I talked with some of the Union representatives. They seemed to be representing the interests of their men and I did not gather that there had been any serious disputes. Yet the management assured me that they had to consider the workers' point of view and that bargaining between the two sides is sometimes quite hard.

We saw something of the welfare connected with the factory. There was a nursery school and *crèche* for women who work in the factory and leave their babies and children there. Here trained nurses and teachers take charge till the mother's shift is over and she can go home. The expense of this is found partly by the factories and partly by the State Department that deals with Welfare. We formed the best possible impression of the child welfare work at this factory.

I next had the opportunity of meeting two professors of Moscow University, both on the side of the 'humanities', the non-scientific side. Here I found a very friendly atmosphere and I was asked to go to the University and address a group of students who were learning English, and some of them were going on exchange visits to England. I spoke to them about my experiences in Russia during the October Revolution and they were spell-bound when I told them that I had seen and spoken to Lenin. It was as if I had had communication with the founder of their religion who was to them a venerated, almost sacred name. But they also seemed to understand when I told them that we in the West had developed institutions based on ideas in which the individual liberty of the citizen was the keystone. It had taken us centuries to develop this, but just as Communism was the basis of their faith, so this was of ours. Altogether the atmosphere was quite different from what I remember forty and more years ago, when 'liberty' to the Communists of 1918 and during the nineteen-twenties and nineteen-thirties was just a synonym for 'capitalist exploitation and liberty of the masses to starve'. Although questions were asked for, I had no hostile ones along these lines now.

In conversation with my two professors, I referred to the Stalin régime and said I could never forgive Stalin for judicially murdering such men as Bukharin, whom I had known personally and knew him well enough to understand that he could not possibly have been a traitor to Russia. It was, I said, just a frame-up because Stalin was jealous of his influence. To my surprise, neither of them said a word in reply to this, and I thought that in the case of one there was a faint nod of approval.

I did not get the same response when I talked to them about the famous book of Pasternak's, *Dr Zhivago*. I said that I knew from personal experience in Russia during the years 1914-1918 that Pasternak in that book was depicting the agonies of uncertainty through which the intellectuals and the professional and middle classes of Russia were passing during those years. They hated Tsarism, but when the Revolution came they hated the crude methods of the Communists. So they were buffeted about between Right and Left. Some joined the Counter-revolution, some joined the Communists, some were forced into the irregular bands of anarchist insurgents that roamed the countryside in those days, some remained unattached to the last. I thought that Pasternak in *Dr Zhivago* had got the tragic position of these people very accurately. But my two professors thought I was wrong. The book was too pessimistic and created the impression that there was a right and a wrong in the whole question. The hero of the story moreover, Dr Zhivago, could not make up his mind. This was not the kind of character one should idealize in the revolutionary situation which existed in Russia in 1917 and 1918. Maybe it was unfortunate that he could not make up his mind, I said, but the fact is that that is what happened because I saw it with my own eyes. The book was a perfect picture of what happened. Personally I had felt much sympathy from the first days of the October Revolution with the Communists (Bolsheviks) because they seemed to me to be the only people who knew their minds and would be able to pull Russia out of the chaos into which she had fallen. They agreed, but thought that those who could not make up their minds in that situation were of no account and so we agreed to differ.

On the subject of the other controversial novel, *Not by Bread Alone*, by Duditseff, I found them more accommodating. The book did show up the evils of bureaucracy and of the upper layers of the Soviet civil service, but they said that Krushchev was altering all that. It would take time, however. We all agreed that the Russian Soviet form of government was something well suited to Russia because the country was so vast and unwieldy that there has always been a tendency among Russians to be disorderly. A strong central government has been a historical necessity for the country since the time of the Mongol invasion in the thirteenth century, and Ivan the Terrible was the first man to realize this and to unify the hitherto chaotic community of the Eastern Slavs.

We also discussed the necessity for strong measures to pull Russia out of her backwardness. We agreed that Russia had not passed through the kind of experience that we and France had in the coming of the Renaissance in art and literature in the sixteenth century and in the Reformation of the Church. All this made Russian history different from ours and its growth more spasmodic than in the West. Communism had performed the necessary function of forcing a backward people out of its lethargy when democratic methods might not have succeeded.

Moscow

There was an Industrial and Agricultural Exhibition more or less permanently open in Moscow, and in due course I went to see it. A student of the University of Frunze, formerly Pishbek, in Turkestan, accompanied me. He had got his degree there and was now taking a further course at Moscow University. While we were at the Exhibition another student, a friend of his, joined us and together we walked through the great halls and buildings which had been erected to show the Russian public in a popular way the great discoveries of science in recent years. The public too was obviously very interested and crowded in to see practical demonstrations of nuclear power production, jet propulsion and even the more prosaic things like the working of an internal-combustion engine. There is little doubt that the Russian public is being rapidly educated to regard the discoveries of science as the most important factor in human life, giving man power over Nature to an unlimited degree. But what interested me most were the houses showing the exhibits from the various Republics of the Union in Asia, particularly in Turkestan, in the Uzbek Republic, in the Republic of Kazakistan and Khirghisia. My companion, the university student who had studied in Frunze, had been in the centre of a Moslem population of that part of Turkestan and they had formerly been largely nomads. I asked him how he got on with these people and he said he got on quite well with the students, who seemed to look on life very much as he did and were anxious to make their careers anywhere where they could find good jobs throughout the Soviet Union. I asked if they mixed socially with the Russians who had gone to live out there. He said there seemed to be a certain barrier between them. Intermarriage between Russians and native Turkestan Moslems was rare, although it did happen among young people sometimes. It did not seem that religion was a barrier. It seemed to be more the customs which grew out of Mohammedanism, the keeping of certain fasts like Ramazan and the family traditions that divided the two races, especially the native peasants from the Russian settlers. My student acquaintance liked his time there, and like all Russians he had no feeling of racial superiority at all. Yet I felt that not all the barriers are down yet between the European Russian and the Moslems of Central Asia. If that is so in the not very strict Moslem areas of Kazakistan and Khirghisia, it is even more so with the much stricter Moslems of Uzbekistan and Tadjikistan which lay farther to the south. Nevertheless, one could see in the Exhibition that considerable progress is being made in irrigation, the starting of processing industries and textile factories in those parts of Asiatic Russia, but Russians are coming in as engineers, technicians, industrial executives and administrators of these countries and in time will become, no doubt, the dominant element in the population. Whatever comes out of this will be very different to our free British Commonwealth.

Both the students were very free in their conversation with me. They were both desperately anxious to visit England. They said openly that they wanted to see what life was like outside Russia. The great trouble for them was finding the money. They could not find it and they would have to be sponsored by some organization. Yet they were very proud of Russia's achievements in the world of science and engineering. The Communist Party did not seem to enter into their calculations. Neither of them were members of it. One of them said that many people joined in order to get better jobs because these would be more likely to come along if they were members. I asked about the position of writers in the Soviet Union. They thought that many were getting tired of writing official propaganda and of gearing their articles and novels to what the official Party line was. Consequently one got people writing now more independently. But there were limits here beyond which one could not go. Also one must be prepared to put up with a hard struggle to make a living. My talk with these two students indicated that they were patriotic Russians, but were striving for a broader outlook on life than the official Communist Party was as yet prepared to allow. All the same, one sensed that free expression of opinion was not frowned on officially quite as much as it had been in the recent past.

During our stay in Moscow, I called on the directors and manager of the Timber Export Trust with which my family business has considerable trade every year. The building is situated in the Kitai Gorod where the old Moscow merchant houses used to be. I remember in 1910 (fifty-one years ago) going to visit an old Moscow business family who had large forests and textile mills and with whom we did business. It was Peter Milutin & Co, and the family concerned was the Bardigins. I was invited to a dinner in old Muscovite style. Everyone crossed themselves before the ikon in the corner of the room before sitting down. We talked about winter sports and bear-hunting. At the office, we talked about much the same things as we do now, the steadiness or otherwise of the markets, the cost of freights in the White Sea and Baltic and so on.

Today when I visited the directors of the big State Trust that controls the export of all timber from the Soviet Union I found that we talked over much the same sort of questions. But now the quality of all timber is so much lower than in the days that I remember forty and fifty years ago. The first Archangel Red and first Petersburg Red was the top of the market, fine grained, knotless deals and the price, enormous for those days, was about one-eighth the price of much inferior timber today. There are very little first qualities now and most timber is lumped together as unsorted.

Today the whole timber trade in Russia is brought under the ownership of the State Trust. It is an enormous concern and very unwieldy. It is hard to get decisions on any matter of business without consultations with other departments, like the Ministry of Trade, the Ministry of National Economy, all of whom have to give their approval to any major project. In the old days you only dealt with one firm, operating of course on a much smaller scale, but decisions could be easily arrived at. On the other hand, the timber trade of Russia today is managed in the interests of the economy as a whole and not in the interests of a few Moscow families as formerly. But the process of management is a long and slow process today.

My wife and I were asked to lunch with the directors and manager. It was very different to the dinner I had had with the Bardigin family forty-nine years ago. It was in the restaurant of the National Hotel and not a well-appointed private house. There were no ikons and no one crossed themselves before sitting down. We toasted each other's countries in a cordial manner and I was much struck how interested our two hosts were in our Royal Family. The Royal baby was expected in three months and they spoke of the Queen with the utmost respect and sympathetic interest. Our two hosts were not Communists, but high officials of the State bureaucracy. They were typical of the vast majority of the Russian people. Patriotic Russians who respect and follow the lead of the Communists without sharing their views.

Although I had seen a good deal of the life and work of the people in Leningrad and Moscow and was to see more in the capital of the Ukraine, I was not altogether satisfied. One cannot see the real Russia unless one gets into the provincial towns and villages. I did later succeed in seeing some of these in the Ukraine, but the Ukraine is a part of Russia with a character and history of its own and not altogether that of Northern or Muscovite Russia which, since the days of Ivan the Terrible, has largely dominated the growth of the Russian nation. Consequently, while I was still in Moscow I conceived the idea of getting permission to visit one of the provincial towns within an easy distance of the capital and my eye fell on Vladimir. During all the years that I had lived in Russia, I had never visited it, and besides being a typical provincial town, it is also the centre of some very interesting and historical churches dating back to the eleventh century. Best of all would it have been if I could have visited one or two of the towns along the banks of the Volga. No one can get a true picture of Russia unless they can see the Volga and the towns and villages along its banks, and I found that, a few weeks before I had arrived in the Soviet Union, the whole length of that famous river, which for months had been open during the summer, was suddenly closed to all foreigners. This sort of thing frequently happens and the reason for the closing of whole areas is always a mystery. The foreign embassies in Moscow do not know the reason. It may be military, it may have something to do with the movement of important machinery and stores. It may be due to the complaint of some traveller that accommodation was not quite as he liked it and the authorities and Intourist are very sensitive on this point. It may be due to any or all of these points. Two things, however, might do something to improve matters in this respect. Intourist should not insist on the best accommodation everywhere for fear of travellers' complaints. One cannot expect the same accommodation in provincial towns as one would get in Leningrad and Moscow. On their part also travellers should, if they want to get to these places, be prepared for second-class fare and accommodation.

Nevertheless, it seemed as if my wife and I were going to be allowed to go to Vladimir. The Intourist told us that it was all right, accommodation was arranged and a car was ready to take us there. We started off in high hopes from Moscow early one morning and planned to be there about eleven o'clock. We passed through dreary Moscow industrial suburbs, small scattered villages of wooden houses and long stretches of dark pine forests. All went well till suddenly a police officer stood in the middle of the road and motioned our driver to stop. The car was directed to a police post by the roadside and the driver and our companion-guide, 'Irma', disappeared inside. They were closeted there for at least forty minutes, at the end of which time they emerged crest-fallen and informed us that we had to return to Moscow. They did not know what had happened, but some authority had apparently decided that we must not be allowed to proceed. So we returned, reached Moscow in the afternoon and immediately set about to enquire what had caused all this.

The affair certainly caused a stir. The Intourist officials were furious and telephone calls were buzzing about Moscow all the rest of the day. The very helpful people in the Inter-parliamentary Union (Russian Branch) came at once to see us. We were told that it was a dreadful mistake and that the police officer would be de-graded, that we could go to Vladimir next day. But our plans and dates had been so upset by this that we decided to call it a day, complete our work in Moscow and go on to Kieff and the Ukraine, as already arranged. Quite obviously the people who had arranged this visit to Vladimir for us were as much upset about all this as we, but it is an example of the sort of thing that can happen to travellers in Russia even today if they try to arrange any visits at all off the beaten track. In Tsarist times much was forbidden, but one could generally get round official obstruction. During the Revolution one could go anywhere if one took food with one and could find a place to stand in the corridor of a train. But today the authoritarian State is efficient and all-powerful and one is reminded suddenly of this, as we were that day. Without a moment's warning, you may be stopped by some department of the State apparatus and the other departments know nothing about it. In our case, some authority had apparently decided that foreigners could not go to Vladimir and did not even inform anyone else, or Intourist would not have arranged the visit. Russia always was a country of surprises and still is, and no traveller who is a little enterprising and wants to do a bit more than the conventional tour must be surprised when something like this happens.

That Intourist and the Inter-parliamentary Union people were particularly annoyed at what had happened is shown by what they did the following day. It was arranged that we should be taken over the Kremlin, that part which was not open normally to the public. There is a part of the Kremlin known as the 'Granovietaya Palata' which contains the hall for the reception of foreign ambassadors and for ceremonial occasions used in the days of the pre-Petrine Tsars. Here Ivan the Terrible in the sixteenth century held court. The place was very well restored in the eighteen-eighties. We were also shown the private apartments of the Tsar and the place where Ivan the Terrible kept his wives. The commandant of the Kremlin, an old general in uniform, received us on the stairs which led to the hall. In contrast to all this, we were then taken to see some of the apartments which are still Government offices, although most of the Government departments are now housed in some of the new skyscrapers which have sprung up in new Moscow. In one of the Government offices is a room specially kept where Lenin used to live and work after the Soviet Government had moved to Moscow in the spring of 1918. It looked very much as I had remembered it, for it was here that I had had a half-hour talk with Lenin in the summer of that year. The prospects of the Revolution were at that time poor. The Germans were still in the Ukraine, shutting off the food supply from North Russia, and the counter-revolutionary White armies were converging on Moscow from Siberia and the Crimea. I marvelled at Lenin's coolness and his faith that Russia was large, and that he could hold out against his enemies in the vast open spaces of the country till the 'Imperialist Powers' cut their own throats in the World War. Then he would deal with his home-bred counter-revolutionary Whites. Looking back on all this, one can see that Lenin's instinct was not far wrong.

While we were in Moscow, we had the good fortune to get tickets for the famous Moscow Art Theatre and to see acted the great Tolstoy novel, *Anna Karenina*. I remember that theatre in the days of Stanislavsky, who started it, and I used to see the Russian classics from Pushkin to Chekhof acted there forty and forty-five years ago. I think that over the years that I have known it, it has altered very little. The Russian genius for acting is as great as ever and seems to me to be best expressed in the extraordinary realism of presentation. One can almost say that there are no stars with the rest of the cast there to spotlight the stars. Everyone in a sense is a star and all are important pieces in the mosaic of the whole play. I know of no other people who bring this out so strongly as the Russians.

As I said in the chapter on Leningrad, I thought that the art galleries and museums there were more impressive than those of Moscow. There is, of course, one exception, and that is the Tretiakoff Gallery in Moscow. It is only for Russian art, starting with the ecclesiastical, mainly ikons of the Middle Ages, passing on through the eighteenth century when modern art started in Russia and the main subjects were portraits of emperors and empresses and the families of the nobility, and then going on through the nineteenth century and the great Russian realist schools of that period. Since the Revolution, the directors of the Gallery have arranged the pictures strictly in consecutive historical periods to show the connection between art and the type of society existing at the time. This is very much in keeping with Marxist-Communist ideas of historical determinism. But actually when I first saw the Gallery in 1910, forty-nine years ago, there was even then that kind of arrangement for the pictures, showing the way Russian art had developed throughout the centuries. It is perhaps a little clearer now than it was then. What strikes one now, if one knows a little Russian history, is that the ecclesiastical art of the Middle Ages persisted right through to the end of the seventeenth century. There was no flourishing school of realist painters, no natural art with a resurgence of the classical tradition as in Western and Southern Europe, nothing corresponding to the art which followed the Protestant Reformation and is so well expressed in the Dutch School of the seventeenth century. For there was no reformation of the Church in Russia in the sixteenth and seventeenth centuries and no artistic renaissance during that period either. The dead hand of mediaeval ideas in religion and art persisted in Russia when in the rest of Europe the flood-gates had opened and new ideas were streaming in. All this comes out when one looks at the Tretiakoff Gallery.

As if to make up for this, however, when the nineteenth century did come, the flood-gates in Russia did open with a vengeance. The great school of Russian realist painters appeared like Riepin, Vereshchagin, Shishkin, Savitsky, Kuindji, Vasnetsoff and Aviloff. They showed the Russian public that art was intimately connected with their daily lives, not with ikons of saints only and not at all with Tsars and aristocrats. I always think that especially impressive of this period are the paintings of Vereshchagin on the wars in Central Asia and the Russo-Turkish war of 1877-78. Here one has an artist who, for the first time, even in Tsarist times, dares to show up war for what it is. For Vereshchagin and others spare one nothing in the portrayal of the gloom and the tragic side of life and the horrors of war. His famous picture 'All quiet on the Shipka Pass' is an example. All this started in the nineteenth century and reached its apex in the last part of it. The still more modern art since the October Revolution simply carries on the tradition of the previous century. There are some quite good painters of scenes in the Civil War between 1918 and 1921. Particularly good in this respect is Grekoff, but even he does not come up to Vereshchagin in my opinion. All these phases of Russian art are to be seen in the Tretiakoff Gallery, arranged in chronological order. The revolutionary régime since 1917 has carried on the tradition and improved the general display of the Gallery, but Soviet artists have produced nothing strikingly new, when you compare them with the giants of the last part of the nineteenth century.

In all Russia's cities and towns one comes up against the statues and portraits of Lenin. Nowhere is one allowed to forget him, and this is specially true of Moscow. Here is his tomb, and beside him lies Stalin. When one goes to pay homage to him, it is on Lenin that one sees the people look. His is the spirit that dominates still. One feels that 'Though dead he speaketh'. Though I met no one in Russia who, like me, had been there at the beginning of the Revolution and had seen him in action, I could sense that a tradition had been handed down. He was the great figure and the guiding hand through those critical years. Perhaps the most moving experience is to go to the Lenin Museum in the Red Square, where there are valuable historical records of his life and career, and at the end one enters a chamber where lies on a cushion his death-mask, draped round by dark purple curtains. Not a sound is to be heard here. There is a deep religious atmosphere as if one was in the presence of a buried saint. Yet he was no saint, but a symbol of the new religion of Russia. Though only a small percentage of the people belong to the new religion, still everyone venerates Lenin, and some who venerate Lenin still stand by the old Russian Orthodox Church which survives and even flourishes in modesty.

CHAPTER V

KIEFF AND THE UKRAINE

Character of the Ukraine and its history; its culture and language; the Ukraine and its relations with Moscow; changes in Kieff; art galleries, theatres and the Ukrainian ballet; fashions and style of dress; hills and parks of Kieff; memories of the First World War; visit to the Ukrainian Ministry of Agriculture; a Russian school in the Ukraine; visit to the agricultural exhibition; visit to museum and Academy of Science; St Sophia and the ecclesiastical monuments of Kieff; mass at St Vladimir on Sunday; the meaning of 'Toska' and 'Prostor'.

HAVING seen the two chief cities of Northern Russia round which the Russian State had been originally built by Ivan the Terrible and his successors in Moscow and by Peter the Great in Leningrad, we next decided to visit Kieff and the Ukraine. This south-westerly part of the old Empire and of the modern Soviet Union is really the oldest part of Russia, where the first beginnings of a State appeared and where the Eastern Slavonic culture began to grow over nine hundred years ago. The Ukraine is a pleasant land, an open rolling plain, much of it fertile, which lies south and west of the great belts of forest and swamp that still cover so much of Central and Northern Russia. Nature in the south-west is kind, just as it is harsh in the east and north. This is reflected also in the people, who in the Ukraine are soft and light-hearted, while the people of the north, the Muscovites, are tough, hard-working and competent. It is no accident that Moscow became the seat of Russian political authority and Kieff became known for picturesqueness and romance. But it must never be forgotten that when Moscow was a collection of fishermen's and fur-hunters' huts, Kieff and the Ukraine were the centre of a flourishing civilization, where the Eastern Slavs first became Christian and built round their Orthodox Church a culture with a language, a writing, a literature and an architecture which was the first to see the light of day in Eastern Europe. The descendants of these Russians today are called Ukrainians.

They were not fated to continue their civilization and culture. It flourished from A.D. 1000 to some way into the thirteenth century. Then a catastrophe overwhelmed it. The great Mongol invasion in

1240 brought hordes of savage horsemen from the steppes of Central Asia sweeping across this fair land and laid it in ruins. When Russian civilization started again some two centuries later, it was brought partly from the north, where the people had taken refuge in forest and swamp and the land was recolonized by the ancestors of the present Ukrainians. Politically and culturally, however, after this catastrophe, a large part of the Ukraine came under the control of the Kings of Poland and the Ukrainian peasants became serfs to Polish landlords. Only after the revolt of Bogdan Khmelnitzky in the seventeenth century and after the battle of Poltawa in 1707, where Peter the Great defeated the Swedes, did the Ukrainians become a partner with the Muscovites and North Russians and since then the two people have grown up together. But the Ukrainians still feel themselves somewhat different from the North Russians. It is a bit like the difference between English and Scots. But perhaps rather more so because the Ukrainians have a language of their own, which belongs to the Slavonic group of languages yet is a quite distinct language from Great Russian. They have a literature of their own too and their architecture, at least in the churches, is quite distinct and more Westerly through Polish influence than in Muscovite Russia. Yet the two people in the modern world take part in the social and economic development of the Soviet Union. All Ukrainians know Russian and many of them serve and work in parts of the Union outside the Ukraine. But they do not forget that they have had a history and tradition of their own. In the more recent past the enemies of Russia in two World Wars and the anti-revolutionary movements after the two revolutions of 1917 have tried to drive a wedge between Muscovite Russians and the Ukrainians. Yet they have not succeeded, because in spite of differences in history and growth, the two people are now thrown together by their geographical proximity as inhabitants of the great East European plain. Their problems of everyday life have become more and more similar.

On arrival in Kieff, we were taken by Intourist guides to an hotel in the centre of the city. We began to look about for ourselves. In some respects the people look much the same as in Moscow and Leningrad. There is certainly much mingling and inter-marrying between Russians and Ukrainians. There are thirty-two million Ukrainians and one hundred and seven million Great Russians, but seven million of these latter live in the Ukraine. About five million Ukrainians also live outside the Ukraine. One hears both languages spoken in the street of Kieff, and spoken about equally. The newspapers one buys in the streets are almost entirely Ukrainian and to me were largely unintelligible. But I found I could with difficulty puzzle out a Ukrainian sentence, for it has always some resemblance to Great Russian. At the same time one has to be careful, for a word may seem the same in Ukrainian and Great Russian and even for that matter in Polish, but one often finds on enquiry that the word which sounds the same in three languages often has quite different meanings. So I had to wait till the Moscow newspapers arrived in the late morning before I could read anything and be sure that I understood it.

I kept on comparing all that I saw in Kieff with what I remembered when I was there first in 1915 during the First World War forty-five years ago. Then there was nothing to tell that the people of Kieff were not all Great Russians. There was no Ukrainian newspaper to be bought. It was, in fact, forbidden to publish them. No Ukrainian books could be got in the shops and Gogol could only be read in Great Russian. Outside the villages one never heard Ukrainian spoken at all. It was the policy of the Tsarist régime in its decline to suppress local nationalist, political and cultural movements, probably in the mistaken idea that in this way it strengthened itself. The Soviet régime, on the other hand, has followed a quite different and much wiser policy. Cultural autonomy is allowed and even encouraged. Ukrainians, Tartars, Georgians, Kazaks, Uzbegs and others are all assisted to have their own newspapers, to publish books in their own languages and have their languages taught along with Great Russian in the schools, and their own theatre and drama.

Of course, in political and many economic matters everything is centralized in Moscow. The principle of the Tsarist régime is continued here with the difference that all the political leaders must now be Communist. Formerly they were chosen from the Imperial family or the nobility. But today in education and in cultural matters full autonomy is allowed and encouraged. In Kieff there is a Ukrainian Government with a local Soviet Parliament dealing with all strictly Ukrainian affairs. Education is entirely in the hands of a local Minister of Education. Agriculture and rural economy has a Minister. Even the large industries have been allowed to run under local government auspices without as much reference to Moscow as before.

In general, when I compared Kieff today with what I had seen fourteen years ago, I could see that, although the city had not changed as much as Moscow and one could still recognize large areas and streets as I had known them then, the main shopping centre, the 'Kreshchatic' had been completely destroyed in the last war and had been now completely rebuilt. Again one could see, as in the new university building in Moscow, a new and somewhat original style of architecture, not now so peculiarly Ukrainian but just Russian. The larger buildings showed signs of a slightly oriental style, like the crenelated walls of the Kremlin and towers with spires on them. In the past Ukrainian church architecture could be distinctly differentiated from the rest of Russia. But that is not so of the secular architecture of today. This is also true of pictorial art. We went to see the Russian and Ukrainian art galleries. With the best will in the world I could not see anything peculiar or original in the Ukrainian picture gallery; nothing in fact that was not there in the collection of Russian paintings in the other gallery. In the Russian picture gallery there was an excellent collection of my favourite Vereshchagin pictures which seemed to have been divided between Moscow, Leningrad and Kieff, so that each of these capitals should have some each of the great Russian works. Of course, one did see painters such as Riepin with his picture of a scene famous in Ukrainian history of the 'Zaparozhny Cossacks' writing a letter to the Sultan. Then there is the Ukrainian artist, Kundjee, whose pictures are devoted to beautiful Ukrainian landscapes with some extraordinary colour effects of sunsets in the fields and villages. These have a definite Ukrainian touch about them.

One could see more distinct features in Ukrainian drama and dancing, different from the rest of Russia. We saw a performance of the Ukrainian Ballet, which is organized directly under the Ukrainian Ministry of Culture. Although the type of dancing has much in common with what one sees in Moscow, Leningrad and other Russian cities, there is a particular Ukrainian flavour in the historical settings of the dances. Many of the dances originate with the famous Ukrainian Cossacks who held the frontier against the Tartars in the sixteenth and seventeenth centuries. This was still further emphasized when we went to see 'Zaporozhetz na Dunayom', an opera by Gulak Artemofsky. The scenes were well set in Ukrainian history and portrayed the life of the 'Zaporozhny Cossacks' carrying on their struggle with the Turks on the shores of the Danube. The Sultan is brought in together with persons prominent in Ukrainian history during the seventeenth century. In the singing and dancing one notices the lively, almost abandoned, spirit of the players which is a feature of this form of Ukrainian art. This reflects the more jovial and light-hearted Ukrainian nature, in contrast to the deeper and more profound nature of art in Muscovite or Great Russia. I had some difficulty in following the programme because everything was written, said and sung in Ukrainian. But I got neighbours to translate words of which I could not spot the meaning and the rest had enough similarity to Great Russian to enable one to follow. Undoubtedly under the Soviet régime those people of the Ukraine who have a special message to give in artistic expression get their chance now as they never did before.

In general looks the people of Kieff differ little from those of Leningrad and Moscow. There is the same indifference to style of dressing and footwear. A dark and often shabby overcoat bound round at the waist with a belt hides what is beneath. In the main there is no attempt to look nice among the women and there appears to be little demand among the men to see style among their women. I thought, however, I could detect among the women a slightly higher number who had good looks than I noticed in Leningrad and Moscow. That may be due to Polish blood and influence, which for centuries was so strong in the Ukraine. Poles, of course, are in general good-looking and dress well. My wife and I amused ourselves counting the number of good-looking women whom we saw during walks in Kieff. We came to the conclusion that the only places where we could be sure of seeing handsome women were on the stage at the theatre, opera or ballet and in the restaurants.

Again as in Leningrad and Moscow in the old days there were well-dressed people among the aristocrats and higher bureaucrats. I remember seeing members of the landlord class in Kieff when I was there in Tsarist times. They always looked prosperous and well. Now the landlords have gone and style and fashion has not yet developed among the people. But a change may be coming. The higher bureaucrats, technicians, artists and singers get high salaries and can afford to dress well. As yet there is no sign of these people developing a sense of dress and style. But there is no economic hindrance to their getting it now. It will be interesting to see if the will is there.

Kieff is now in parts at least a beautiful city. It has a superb site. No town in European Russia has anything like it. It is built on and round a series of small hills stretching some three miles along the right bank of the River Dnieper. This is one of the big rivers of Southern Russia and a great artery of trade and commerce between the Black Sea and the interior of the country. Important industries are situated on the left bank of the river at Kieff and there is a lively traffic in which trains of barges with tugs and some larger motor vessels are seen plying up and down the river. On the right bank are the rounded hills from the top of which a fine view can be obtained eastwards across the great Russian plain for anything from fifty to eighty miles. These hills are now largely covered by public parks. I remember them during Tsarist times in the First World War. There was a prisoner-of-war camp on one of them and I remember when I was in Kieff in the spring of 1915 getting into conversation one day with some Austrian prisoners-of-war. The frontier with Austria was some 200 miles to the west and Kieff was a transfer depot for them. I remember being struck by the fact that no one interfered with my talking to the Austrians, although there were some Russian sentries about and they saw us talking. Altogether the war at that time and in that part of Europe seemed a somewhat desultory affair. After the Second World War when I was in Kieff in 1945 I again remember prisoners, this time Germans. They were not being repatriated but were being held to do work in helping to reconstruct war-damaged Russia. There was no Geneva Convention on prisoners-of-war between Russia and Germany. The Russians, being the victors, did what they liked with the German prisoners. I saw them being put to work to level the ground, make paths and roads, plant trees and shrubs on the hills of Kieff. I could now see the results of their work, although the people of Kieff also had a large share in it. This has brought it about that Kieff has a wonderful series of public parks on this fine site overlooking the Dnieper. If the First World War was desultory as far as Kieff was concerned, the Second World War was not. The Austrian prisoners in the First World War had a slack time. The Germans in the Second World War certainly had not. But in the meantime Kieff had suffered greatly. After the October Revolution came the Civil War between Russian Reds and Whites, in which Ukrainian Nationalist armed forces also played a rôle, joining first one side then the other and sometimes fighting on their own. Kieff changed hands many times and finally was occupied by the Germans for some six months, then by the North Russian Communists, then by the Poles under Pilsudsky and finally by the united Ukrainian and North Russian Communists. One feels that the uncertainties are now over.

I visited some Ukrainian Government offices in Kieff and had one particularly useful interview with important people in the Ministry of Agriculture. Since the Ukraine grows a large part of all the wheat and dairy produce of European Russia, the Ministry of Agriculture is a very important Government department. I was astonished at the frankness of those with whom I talked there. In Moscow one does not find anyone in Government offices or in the State Trading Trusts who is ready to admit faults and weaknesses, certainly not to a foreigner. But I found that in the Ukraine there was a much freer atmosphere. When I congratulated one of the Ministers whom I met on the improvements that I had noticed in the state of Ukrainian agriculture since I was there last, he said that they were not at all satisfied, that they had a long way to go yet and that Ukrainian agriculture was still very backward. I had just returned from a visit to a village and collective farm and had been giving him my impressions. But he was quite open about it; the state of Russian agriculture was not what it should be. I noticed this sort of frankness during several interviews I had with Ukrainian officials in Kieff and formed the impression that the Communist Party has not got such a hold on the people as it has in the cities and towns of the north. This again is rather characteristic of the happy-go-lucky Ukrainian nature. Also it is frequently noticeable that the farther you go away from Moscow, the less single-minded and forceful and the more tolerant Communists seem to be.

We saw one instance of how the North Russians give an example of efficiency to their Ukrainian cousins. We went to see a primary school for Russian children who are not Ukrainian but who live in Kieff. These children do not need to learn Ukrainian, since their parents may not always be going to live there and may go back to work in North or East Russia. So it is desirable that they should have their own schools separate from those where instruction goes on in both languages. We got the best possible impression of this school, which took children up to eleven. The bias was obviously towards science even at that age. All sorts of equipment for demonstrations in the elementary laws of physics was there. The children's powers of observation were being stimulated and they were being prepared for specialization in their higher education. One wondered perhaps if they were not stimulating specialization a little too early. The atmosphere of this school was excellent. The children made a great noise and enjoyed themselves during the break, but the moment the bell rang there was complete silence and everyone went off to his or her classrooms quietly. They were perfectly mannered, respected their teachers but did not seem afraid of anyone.

I found in Kieff an Agricultural Exhibition in a public park on the edge of the city. It is more or less permanently there, though closed from time to time to alter the exhibits. The Ukrainian Government find the cost of this to stimulate public interest in agriculture among the townspeople and among the peasants, who come in in parties from the village to see the latest machinery and cultivation methods and the different types of livestock there. The latter were particularly interesting, for one could see all the different breeds of cattle, sheep and pigs which are now to be found in the farms and villages of the Ukraine. What has happened in the Ukraine is very similar to what has happened in North Russia. Each part of the country has a native breed of cattle, small, dun-coloured and hardy, but not a very good milk or meat producer. In the Ukraine this small animal is called the 'Lebedinskaya', but there is a similar one in North Russia. The policy over several decades now has been to cross this hardy native with the larger and higher quality animals from Western Europe. Most popular in this respect have been the Ziementhal cattle from Switzerland. The result of this cross is a good dairy type of cow.

Other crosses which have been made are with the Herefords and are known in the Ukraine as the Bielogolovaya ('White-faced'). The Friesians are also to be found both in the Ukraine and North Russia. They were originally imported to the White Sea in the days of Peter the Great and are called Holmogorsky. They apparently are fairly pure Friesians and have not been crossed with the small native animal. Looking at the Agricultural Exhibition at Kieff, one gets the impression that in the Ukraine at least there is a good selection of both dairy and beef cattle to provide stock for the collective farms, but whether the most economical use is made of them is a matter that I shall deal with in the next chapter on the collective farms.

While I was at the Agricultural Exhibition, I found a long shed which had in it a number of horses. Quite obviously the horse is still used in agriculture in Russia. But there were also racing horses which are being bred in Russia. I saw types of horses very similar to our Shires and others which were good thoroughbreds with Arab blood in them. While I was there, one of the Directors of the Show who deals specially with the horses heard that I was English, came to me and showed me round himself, taking me everywhere and describing carefully the history of each horse, its pedigree and where it came from. He thought that because I was English I must be fond of horses, and he was right in that. But I was impressed by the fact that he gave so much time to me and was so very friendly. He wanted to know also about our experiences in England with cattle like Herefords and Friesians which we export to the Continent of Europe for crossing. He knew a lot about our types of cattle and clearly wanted to know more with the object of improving their stock. But there was something more than deliberate friendliness here. This was a good example of the impulsive open-heartedness of Russians which always bursts out when the crust of officialdom is broken down.

While I was in Kieff, I found that the museum of the Ukrainian Academy of Science was open again and much enlarged. Last time I was there it was closed and had been damaged in the war. But it was now restored and one of the professors took me round. They are doing important research work on the origin and nature of the black earth soil of the Southern Ukraine and are trying to solve the problem of how it came to be formed in the post-glacial era. Research is also continuing in the burial mounds of the Ukraine in the attempt to know more of the early inhabitants of the East European plain. In the Zoological Section of the Academy I found that the European Bison (*Bison bonasus*) is now no longer to be found in a wild state. Until the last war there were a few herds still in the big forest belt lying south of Briansk on the borders between the Ukraine and

Muscovite Russia. But during the war they were hunted down for meat. Now, however, there is a herd of about one hundred of them kept in a reserve on the upper Oka River about eighty miles from Moscow. The Ornithologists at the museum were also doing research work into wild duck and geese and wanted to make contact with our Wild Fowl Trust. I found the Professors of the Academy of Science very anxious to get in touch with our natural scientists and archaeologists in Britain because they have been cut off for so long by the war and then by the Stalin terror period, when any contact with a foreigner, however harmless, was regarded as high treason and a mark of the 'Fascist beast'.

No one can visit Kieff without seeing the ancient ecclesiastical monuments, the most numerous and of the most historical interest in all Russia and, indeed, in all Eastern Europe. The Soviet régime has not only opened them to the public, but has made most valuable researches on them and has done a lot to enrich our knowledge of this great heritage of the past. Some of the monuments, like the Cathedral of St Sophia, are now museums. But others, like St Vladimir, have been handed back to the Church and services are regularly held there before packed congregations. Also the Monastery of the Caves ('Pechersky Lavra') has been handed back to the order of monks who originally lived there and the monks are allowed to keep the offerings given by the pilgrims who come in considerable numbers to pay their devotions to the saints of former centuries who lie buried there. Within the walls of the monastery there is a museum of ecclesiastical art and the ruins of the Cathedral of the Assumption. It was originally built in the twelfth, but was restored and largely rebuilt in the eighteenth century. It is the only casualty of an ancient building that Kieff suffered from in the last war when during the German occupation it was blown up under obscure circumstances.

The Communist régime of Russia is much interested in preserving ecclesiastical monuments. Architecture, like art in general, is regarded by Marxists as a reflection of the economic state of society existing at that period. Therefore, the Soviet régime has spent considerable sums of public money in researching on and restoring these monuments, and not the least they have done is in connection with the Cathedral of St Sophia. When I first saw it in 1915 in Tsarist times it looked nothing like as beautiful and interesting as it does today. With the exception of the famous mosaic work of the Madonna in the apse over the altar, done by Greek masters in the eleventh century, there was little else to see on the walls. The Soviet experts have, however, now uncovered the greater part of the walls round the four Byzantine arches and in the main and side galleries. As a result, the whole Cathedral is one large exhibition of wall paintings dating from the eleventh and twelfth centuries, the richest store of its kind in Eastern Europe with the exception of Constantinople. Damp and neglect at various times have damaged and even destroyed some of the figures in the paintings and frescoes. These have been re-painted by well-known artists of recent times like Vrubel, who specialized in this kind of work.

The historical importance of the Cathedral of St Sophia at Kieff lies in the fact that it is the great symbol of the advance of the Eastern Slavs from a primitive pagan community to their entry into the culture of the Byzantine Greeks and of the Orthodox form of Christianity. Vladimir, the Prince of Kieff, first sent ambassadors to the Byzantine Emperor and in 988 accepted Orthodox Christianity. His son, Yaroslav the Wise, won in 1036 a victory over the nomadic tribe of the Pechenegs, the precursors of the Tartars two centuries later. To commemorate his victory he built St Sophia, sent to Byzantium for Greek architects and artists and modelled the building as an almost exact replica on a smaller scale of the famous Cathedral of St Sophia built by Justinian in Constantinople. Fundamentally it is not a Russian building at all but a Greek one, and is so interesting because it shows that Russian civilization is quite separate from that of the Roman Catholic West or from the Islamic civilization of the Orient. It is, in fact, a world of its own between these other two worlds, based on the Eastern European forms of Greek Orthodox Christianity. This is the fundamental reason why, though Russia has been geographically in Europe, she has never been culturally part of the Western world. She has always gone her own way separate from the West with its Roman traditions and from the Middle East with its Perso-Arab influences. But it is more complicated than this. For this form of culture based on Kieff and the Orthodox Church was subjected to great trials. In 1240 the Mongol commander, Batu Khan, swept across the Ukraine towards Central Europe. Kieff was destroyed and the inhabitants massacred or fled. St Sophia lay deserted for nearly four hundred years. A visitor in 1569 wrote of it as being 'the home of wild beasts and of weeds and falling into ruins'. In 1632, in response to a Ukrainian national movement led by Bogdan Khmelnitsky, Peter Mogil became Metropolitan of the Orthodox Church in the Ukraine. He set to work to restore Orthodox Christianity as opposed to the Roman Catholic form introduced by the Poles. Bogdan Khmelnitsky also set himself up to expel the Poles from the Ukraine. In 1654 he entered Kieff in triumph and the union between the Ukraine and Great Russia was declared. During the rest of the seventeenth century, work proceeded on the Cathedral of St Sophia. Its completion was delayed by fire and it was not fully restored till 1707, in which year Peter the Great was received by the people of Kieff after his victory over the Swedes at Poltawa. In the restoration the old Byzantine walls remained with the frescoes and the mosaics, but the roof and the cupolas were all new. These, instead of being Byzantine domes, were of the kind known as 'Ukrainian baroque'. The influence of the Poles and of the Roman Catholic Church is here to be seen today in the Ukraine. The same kind of towers and cupolas can be seen all over Poland, Austria and even as far south as Italy today, and they show that Western influence had during the period of the Polish hegemony in the Ukraine penetrated there and left its mark. This also distinguishes Ukrainian church architecture today from that of Muscovite and North Russian church architecture. The Greek half-sphere is replaced by the pear-shaped cupola. But the original Greek influence in the Cathedral of St Sophia in Kieff is still very strong. It is probably best seen in the mosaics. There are two very fine mosaics of the Madonna and one very large face of Christ, the All Powerful, or 'Pantokrator', in the central dome. They are typical of Byzantine religious art during the best period of the tenth to the twelfth centuries. The subjects portrayed here have that unearthly look on their faces which no one but the Byzantine Greeks ever seem to have got either before or since to the same extent.

The last Sunday we were in Kieff my wife and I went to the service at the Orthodox Cathedral which is in use and is called St Vladimir. It is quite modern and was built in 1882 in pure Byzantine style somewhat along the lines of what St Sophia originally was. On the steps of the Cathedral were a large number of old men and women begging for alms. My wife was rather shocked at seeing these in the Soviet Union, where everything is supposed to be done for the workers. I made enquiries about this and came to the conclusion that these old people do this because they think that the Church and not the State is the place where public assistance can and should be sought. They would be perfectly entitled to receive three hundred roubles a month (roughly £10) from the Soviet State and go and live in one of the homes set aside by the Ministry of Public Welfare in all towns throughout the Union. But they do not recognize this and being religious old people they stick to what they have always believed, that the Church lays down the giving of alms and charity to the poor, so they go on as they always have and the Soviet State leaves them alone.

Inside the Cathedral that morning there was a crowd of people of all ages and both sexes devoutly praying and singing as their fathers once did. Waves of emotion swept over the congregation from time to time, as some very solemn act was performed by the priest in the mysterious background behind the screen or iconostas.

The Orthodox Church certainly does appeal to wide sections of the Russian and Ukrainian public still. Much of its power seems to rest in the atmosphere of mystery that surrounds the performance of the Mass, a symbol of the mystery of life and death, which no one can explain but only feel.

Before we left Kieff I went with a young Ukrainian woman, who had been delegated to show me the Kieff parks, to the top of one of the hills of Kieff. The view was very fine. The vast spaces of Russia create in one a feeling that I find it hard to describe. I am sure that it affects the Russians themselves and forms an element in their character. The rulers of Russia today believe that man through science can dominate matter and create a world of plenty and happiness. They have taught the youth of Russia that this is so. The young woman guide who was with me believed what her leaders had taught her. Yet I am satisfied that today this is not the real spirit of Russia. It is only a temporary reaction against the traditional spirit of Russia caused by the breakdown of the old Tsarist régime. Everything had been thrown out whether it was good or bad. It seemed that my companion was not really satisfied with the new philosophy. It was all right up to a point, but it had something lacking. 'The Russian is always feeling Toska,' she said, as we discussed this feeling of dissatisfaction with life. What is Toska? I thought. It is almost untranslatable and is something very Russian. Perhaps one could call it the longing for something that is not there, that you know never will be there but that you must go on longing for. Hence your thoughts are permeated by a slight sadness and a sense that fate will in the long run impede your strivings.

We talked about the fate of the Principality of Kieff, how it had flourished for three hundred years and then was struck down by inexorable fate in the form of the Mongol invasion. She thought that could not happen now. Couldn't it, I said; what about the H-bomb? She was silent. We looked out from the park across the Dnieper. The immensity of the Russian plain extending round us to the horizon on all sides dominates one. It dominated me and I think her too, for in the last resort she was a Russian first and a Communist second. I thought of the words of the Ukrainian national poet, Gogol. 'The power of vastness embraces me and reflects itself in my inmost depths. It is in "Prostor" that limitless thought is born. Is not this the place for the folk heroes of Russia?' 'Prostor' is another untranslatable Russian word but might perhaps be held to mean the conception of illimitable distances which impress on Man his limitations in the presence of powers mightier than he. And from this one's mind can move on to reflect that no one can attain on earth all that he longs for. The struggle between Good and Evil is eternal, as the ancient Persians were the first to discover. Gogol saw this, Tschaikowsky told of it in his symphonies, so did Dostoiefsky in his great novels, and so do the Russian people feel it, or at least a large part of them, even now, for this is the real philosophy that makes them at times hesitant, uncertain of themselves and aware that Communism does not give them all the truth, though it gives some. Does not this explain why the Orthodox Church still has so many adherents and why young Russians are still searching for the truth and causing some anxiety to their Communist leaders. But truth cannot be found in one philosophy completely. For Goethe said in *Faust*, Part II, 'I love him who yearns for the impossible.'

CHAPTER VI

AGRICULTURE AND THE UKRAINIAN VILLAGE

Memories of old Polish aristocracy in Ukraine; I visit a landed estate near front against Austria; life in Ukrainian village before Revolution; end of Polish régime; reasons for collectivization and the second agrarian revolution; I visit collective farm after Second World War; I visit same farm fourteen years later; I see big changes; talk with farm manager; surplus labour and machinery; standard of farming efficiency; financial results and standard of living of peasants; farming methods and livestock rearing; yields per acre and output per cow; visit to peasant's house and supper with family; private holdings of peasants; divided loyalties; future of collective farming; expansion of the Eastern Slavs; the Pripet Marshes; we leave Russia.

I HAVE been in the Ukraine three times; once in 1915, forty-five years ago, and then in 1945, fifteen years ago, and again last autumn. On all three occasions I visited villages and farms. I can, therefore, look back and note what changes have taken place over nearly half a century. Before I describe what I saw last autumn and fifteen years ago, I must first reflect how I remember farming and country life in the Ukraine when I was there first in Tsarist times.

It happened in this way. The First World War was on and I was War Correspondent for the *Manchester Guardian* and was visiting the Russian front against Austria in Galicia in April 1915. On my way to the front, I stayed at Kieff and had the good fortune to meet a Polish landlord who had estates in the Western Ukraine near Lvov (Lemberg). His father had come over to England as an exile after the first Polish revolt against Russia in 1831 and had married an English lady. He became British, entered the army and served in the Crimean War. His son, the gentleman whom I met, married a Polish heiress who had estates near Lvov. He was seventy-five when I met him in Kieff in 1915. I found his position difficult. He was still a British subject. He disliked the Tsarist régime in Russia which had persecuted his father and had suppressed all Polish nationalist movements. He was enthusiastic about the Austrian Empire and the Emperor Franz Joseph who had granted liberty and autonomous government to the Poles of Galicia. This was part of the Austrian Empire north of the Carpathians and inhabited by both Poles and Ukrainians (the latter also called Ruthenians). His sympathies were, therefore, very divided. He loved England and Austria and both were at war with each other, and England was an ally of Tsarist Russia whom he hated. This was typical of the sort of dilemma the Poles had been in for generations, so tragically partitioned between Austria, Prussia and Russia.

But equally tragic was the fact that these Polish landlords were becoming anachronisms in a land where all the peasants and retainers were Ukrainian. They performed no useful function in society, were receivers of rents which they spent in Paris or the Riviera and their peasants belonged to another nationality and religion, Ukrainian and Orthodox or Uniate.[1] The main interest, therefore, of the Ukrainians was to free themselves from the Poles both nationally, in religion, socially and economically.

Meeting this Polish gentleman again in Lvov a week later after I had met him in Kieff, he invited me to come to his estate some miles to the north-west of the city. The Austrian and Russian armies were entrenched some distance to the west and we went there in order that he might get some of his former possessions away to safety, while I was anxious to see what these Polish landed estates in Galicia were like.

I found a completely feudal atmosphere there, but one where everyone knew his place and complacently accepted his or her status in society. I found a country house with extensive gardens and shrubberies, a park, a forest, a home farm and a village with wide latifundias or open farm land worked by the peasants and stretching for some miles around. The farming was rather primitive.

My host had the manners and habits which existed in aristocratic and conservative society in Western Europe through a large part of what may be called Victorian times. He spoke slowly and deliberately, dined at 5.0 p.m., sat long over his port and was served by a number of retainers who received no wages, but everything including their food and clothing was found for them. My host apologized that his hospitality could not be more lavish, but it was war-time, the two armies were facing each other and this estate was in the war zone. He had had Russian soldiers in his house and they had pilfered many things. He had not got all the food he would have liked to provide. I enquired about the peasants who were not his household retainers. Some of them worked for him on his home farm and were paid partly in wages and partly in kind. The farm was suffering because the Russian Army had requisitioned much of the livestock. The other peasants had less to lose. They worked on the open fields and paid

[1] These were Orthodox in ritual but accepted the authority of the Pope.

him rent in the form of part of their produce such as corn and cattle each year. He had to arrange to sell their produce. The peasants lived very simply and made their own clothes, but they had little to fall back on if there was a bad harvest. They then were dependent on him for charity. The whole set-up was completely patriarchal. It worked, but the peasants, if not in law, were in fact tied to the soil and to the person of the landlord.

But I felt that change was in the air even then. The late Prime Minister of Russia, M. Stolypin, had been working at a plan to give the peasants their own land, enable them to buy out their landlords with State credit and then to have further credits for improvements. I gathered that the idea was being considered also in Austrian Poland where this estate normally was before the war.[1]

Meanwhile war had supervened, Stolypin had been murdered and for the time being all plans of that kind were dropped. When the war ended three years later in revolution both in Austria and Russia, all these estates were swept away, the peasants took the land for themselves and the rule of the Polish landlords which had lasted for centuries was now over. I saw the system at its last gasp. It was dying, and the thunder of the guns which we heard every night on the front near that Polish estate in Galicia was heralding a new era for the peasants of the Ukraine. The Russian and Austrian Empires were going down in the holocaust of war. When I next went to the Ukraine, everything was very different.

I went to Kieff in the autumn of 1945 just after the Second World War. In the intervening years the peasants had got their land when the Revolution had swept the Russian and Austrian Governments away and with them the Polish and Russian landlords. But in Russia now under the Communist régime of Stalin and in Poland under the Communist régime that followed later in the Second World War, the peasants had been forced to give up their individual small farms and amalgamate them into a collective system in which the land was not only owned but also farmed in common. This was the second agrarian revolution which was more fundamental even than the revolution that had removed the landlords. In Central and Northern Russia it was not such an innovation as in the Ukraine. In the former areas of Russia, the peasants had for centuries held their land in common, although they farmed their holdings individually. But every few years a council of all the peasants in the village would meet and distribute their land so that each peasant should have different land and should share the good and the bad soils. In the Ukraine, how-

[1] The reason why I was able to be in Austrian territory at this time was because the Russian Army had defeated the Austrians in September 1914, and had occupied this part of Galicia.

ever, the Stolypin land reforms and the creation of peasant proprietorship had already begun to make some progress before the war and the Revolution. Consequently, the forcible collectivization of farming was a greater shock to the peasants there than in Central and Northern Russia. But Stalin knew that war with Germany was probable for a second time. If Russia was to resist Hitler, she must have more equipment and heavy industry. If she was to have these industries, she must have more food. The peasants, therefore, must produce more, and farming must become more efficient with more machinery. Small peasant holdings could not carry out the change to higher production quickly enough, for time was pressing. So Stalin took the plunge and forced the collective system on to the peasants of Russia at the cost of great social convulsion, some loss of life and enormous loss of livestock.

I had attempted when I was in Kieff in 1945 to see something of what had happened during these years. I had asked to see a collective farm not in a show place to which foreign visitors had often in the inter-war years been taken. I asked to go to one in the poorer sandy country on the edge of the forest belt to the north-west of Kieff and in the direction of Zhitomir. It was arranged for me to see this and I spent a day and a night there. But it was difficult to make any estimate of how successful the collective farm had been because the country had recently been devastated by war. The German Army had advanced across the Ukraine and the Russians had engaged in a scorched earth policy. When the Russian Army was victorious at Stalingrad and returned, the German Army withdrew and it engaged in another scorched earth policy. So in 1945 I saw a collective farm on which there was not much in the way of livestock or implements, but only the beginning of peace-time reconstruction.

I returned last autumn to Kieff and asked if I could see the same farm that I had seen in 1945. I described it to Intourist people in Kieff and gave its name and its position on the map. Within twenty-four hours they had found it and a car was put at our disposal at once to go there. So one day in October 1959 we passed along the highway between Kieff and Zhitomir through the country that Gogol loved so well and where Pushkin wrote *Quiet Ukrainian Nights*. The level of the great plain of Eastern Europe rose and fell in giant waves. Herds of cattle and flocks of geese were grazing over common pastures attended by youths. It was the kind of scene that could be observed anywhere east of Poland and west of the Central Asian desert. Areas of forest were passed, dark blocks of pine, the source of fuel for villages in the winter. Here and there were marshes and woodland glades, the abode of the heron and the wild duck.

We stopped on the main road and went down a side lane reaching a

5 Kieff—River Dnieper and statue of St Vladimir

Country house of Polish aristocrat in Ukraine, 1915

6 Ukrainian peasants and retainers at landlord's country house on Feast Day, 1915

Collective Farm in Ukraine—house for public gatherings and entertainment

large placard which informed us, both in Ukrainian and Russian, that this was the collective farm called 'The First of May'. When I was there last everything was open. All trees had been cut and the houses were exposed to the blasts of Heaven. Now they were surrounded by trees and shrubs planted over the last fourteen years. Some houses had been burned in the war, but had now been rebuilt. There was a new playing-field and a new 'House of Culture' where plays are given and lectures and dances take place. The secondary school had been added to and a memorial had been erected to those in the village who had died in the war.

We were received by the manager of the collective farm who was elected by all the peasants. He was responsible for the administration and there was a treasurer to keep the accounts. Each collective farm had its own independent finances and administration, but, of course, they were much dependent upon the State in the form of the Ukrainian Government, who advanced them money and provided for their machinery, equipment and capital works. Fourteen years ago the then manager had apologized to me for the apparent poverty of the farm and village. In those days it looked indeed as if, in the words of Alexei Tolstoy, Ivan the Terrible and the 'Wrath of God' had passed over the face of Russia. Today the manager had a different tale to tell.

I asked the manager for the figures on production, income and general policy. The area of the collective farm is now 3,100 hectares,* which was more than it was, since it had absorbed another small neighbouring Collective. 2,600 hectares of this was cultivated and the rest was meadow, marsh and forest which belonged to the Collective. There were 700 families in the Collective, so that if one took an average of two workers to each family, that would mean one man for every four acres. Compare the average well-managed farm in England employing one man for every fifty acres! I had not been long in the place before I noticed, as I had fourteen years ago, that in every work brigade, either working at the mill, mixing fodder or mucking out, there were a number of men standing by not working and only starting work when some of the others stopped. I found that there were nine tractors on the farm and seven combines against two tractors and no combines in 1945. Labour-saving machinery seemed of little value with all that amount of labour about. Its only use was that it enabled field work to be got through quickly while weather conditions were suitable. But it must increase the amount of people who are not fully employed but who yet stay on in the village.

Judging from these collective farms, the type of farming is far less efficient than in Western Europe or the United States. The out-

* 1 hectare = 2·47 acres

put per man is low, but not lower than in Eastern Europe generally. Actually it is probably higher than in Poland or Yugoslavia. But many more people are on the land than are necessary having regard to the machinery now in use. Yet the towns and industries of Russia need food in increasing quantities at reasonable prices. How can the hundred and one activities of Russia's modern science and engineering be supported without increasing food from the land? It was clear to me that if what I saw on this collective farm is typical of the rest of Russia, over the last fourteen years there has been an increase in in the output of food but at a considerable cost in high overheads per man and per acre, far higher in fact than in Western Europe and America. There would be on these farms a large economic reserve if fewer families had to be supported on them and a fuller use was made of labour-saving machinery.

I was given the figures for the gross income of the farm, which was in 1958 4,200,000 roubles as against 1,000,000 roubles in 1951. Today running expenses come to about 3,000,000 roubles, which includes repayment over three years for machinery and equipment advanced to the farm by the Government and bought on easy terms. A ten per cent. tax also is paid to the Government on profits. This leaves a nett income of 1,200,000 roubles. With 700 families on the Collective that means an average of about 1,700 roubles per family, which, at the tourist rate of exchange, comes to about £60 a year. This is the dividend of the Collective which each householder receives. He also receives the amount in cash which he earns for each hour that he works in the brigades on the farm. This may vary according to the amount of work done. The standard of living does not seem bad for East European peasants and must be far greater than in the times of the old landlords and also above that of fourteen years ago when the country was recovering from the war.

When I cast my mind back and remembered what I had seen on the Polish landlord's estate near Lvov in 1915, I could see there was no comparison with today. The life of the peasant in a village may mean simple fare, but they are at least not dependent on the charity of one man, like they were when I was there forty-five years ago. Services rendered are now paid for in cash. The first agrarian revolution which got rid of the landlords cleared the ground. The landlords had performed no useful function. They, like the old Irish landlords, were not partners with the peasants as the landlords in England have always been with the farmers. They were fathers of a family and could do as much or as little as they liked. For any improvement in farming that system had to go. But has the collective system of farming caused a big advance in standards of living and efficiency? As regards standards of living, there has undoubtedly

Agriculture and the Ukrainian Village

been an advance, though not perhaps spectacular. As regards increased agricultural efficiency, there has also been an advance on what I had seen fourteen years ago on this collective farm. But then, of course, the whole country was suffering from the effects of the war. The agrarian history of Russia has always been chequered. After the October Revolution private landlordism had hardly gone when civil war devastated the countryside. In the Ukraine there was the Polish invasion and then the invasion of Hitler in the Second World War. The countryside of Russia, especially in the Ukraine, has only had a chance to recover and develop its agriculture in the course of the last ten years. What has been achieved in this time?

There had been considerable additions to buildings at this collective farm in the last fourteen years and a great increase in livestock. But the number of people looking after them had increased too. I found the livestock building had rather more than doubled. The big cattle-shed was more than twice as large and now houses 300 cows and about 100 calves as against 100 cows and not more than 30 calves in 1945. There were 1,600 pigs as against a few hundred then, and two large pig houses had been erected. There were 700 sheep which I did not see and 6,000 poultry. In addition to a mill, which had been enlarged, they now had a silo in which they were storing chaffed straw. They did not seem to have made grass silage, although they grew lucerne. They also had a new fodder-mixing machine in which they were pulping potatoes and mixing it with meals for the pigs. The machinery seemed to be rather dirty and the place needed cleaning up a lot. The pigs, however, seemed to be in fair condition and the bacon I tasted seemed excellent. All liquid manure from the pig houses drained into a sump and the liquid was taken daily to a heap and mixed with compost for the land in the spring. The method seemed excellent.

The yield of wheat in the harvest of 1959 at this farm was 21 zentners per hectare, which is about ten hundredweight to the acre. The average yield for the whole Ukraine was nine hundredweight to the acre. The yield of maize was about seventeen hundredweight to the acre on this farm. The general yield per acre both for wheat and maize made poor showing as against the yields in Britain and the United States.

Milk production fluctuates during the season and it is aimed to get the calves in the spring and summer. Winter milk production does not appear to be very heavy and there is no attempt to keep production even throughout the year. The figure I got for milk yields was for the whole year. It worked out at 9,371 gallons for 250 acres. If one works that out in figures for a good dairy farm in Great Britain, the result would be on an average 21,529 gallons per

250 acres. So here again the output is low compared to the West. In the cow-house there were concrete tying-up stands with a drainage system. All milking was by hand. The litter used was sand and sometimes sawdust. There were no washing-down stands with water, because I was told they wanted to keep the cow droppings for solid manure. In general I had the impression that the dairy would not pass our Milk and Dairies Regulations. There were sixty girls to look after three hundred cows and calves, that is one person per five cows. Compare with the parlour system in England which enables one man to attend to thirty-five cows. All this indicated that though efficiency has increased greatly since the old feudal days and also on the immediate post-war situation, it is still pretty low compared with the West.

The general standard of living of the Ukrainian peasant in the rather poorer soil of the North Ukraine can be seen by our experiences in this village. Fourteen years ago, when I visited it, a peasant in this village had entertained me to tea and supper. When he heard that I was in the village again, he sent to invite my wife and me to come again. There was the thatched cottage as before, but peeping out from behind fruit trees which had since been planted. Inside everything looked the same. The peasant and his wife were older, the little girl was now married and had two children, but lived with the parents. No longer were shirts and blouses made at home. Only window curtains were made by the wife and embroidered with Ukrainian patterns. The house was spotlessly clean and all clothes were now bought. There were no ikons or religious pictures on the walls, but there was also no picture of Lenin or Stalin. There was one of Krushchev, however. Fourteen years ago I had been given a good meal, but twelve hours' notice of my coming had been given. I suspected then that the village had been ransacked for that meal, but today notice was only three hours. Yet in that time the house was able to provide everything from the allotment including eggs, sausages, cheese, chicken and fruit. Life was certainly easier now. The only thing from outside was wine and vodka, and my wife and I had to do our share of drinking these. Many toasts were drunk, including one to Anglo-Russian friendship, and the atmosphere was genuinely and sincerely friendly. I asked my host if anyone ever wanted to leave the collective farm and he said no. Everyone accepts it now because if you were not in it, you would not get the advantages of all being together, and these were considerable with Government support and credits. Having said this, however, the old peasant came out in him. He said he remembered the days of the landlords before the Revolution. Now, he said, we have the State in place of the landlords. But then he said philosophically, 'Someone must give orders.'

I felt that my peasant host, though he was no doubt sincere in his statement that collective farms have an advantage in technical help and in the possibility of greater efficiency in working, nevertheless had a secret hankering after farming on his own. He spoke with such enthusiasm about his private holding that I felt that this was where his real interest lay. No doubt he did his work with the 'labour brigade', earned his wages there and got his annual dividend from the profits of the collective farm. But his real affection was for the few pigs and calves that he was rearing on his own, those fruit trees that he had planted, that vegetable patch and that half-acre of millet which he was growing to feed his household. Like all other members of the Collective, he had four acres of land of his own. He could grow what he liked there, sell it to any consumer he liked and pass the land on to his son when he died, if his son decided to stay a member of this Collective. He had to pay 363 roubles a year for this land in tax to the State, and it could be paid in cash. This was equal to about £12 a year or £3 an acre. But there were no other charges and that tax had been reduced. When I was there last fourteen years ago, he was paying 800 roubles, or £26, a year, and most of that had to be paid in kind, namely produce taken off the holding. This rankled very much, as I remember at the time, and I found that Mr Krushchev had made himself quite popular by reducing this tax and by making it payable in money.

It gave my host much pleasure to show me round his holding, inspect his pigs and calves and admire his fruit trees. Actually I remembered when I was there last that they had just been planted and now they were in bearing. All along the outskirts of the village between the cottages and the wide cultivated lands of the collective farm were the strips of four-acre holdings of the peasants. I walked over some of them and they all showed that much care and attention was being paid to them. Since it was autumn and the crops were off, the peasants had agreed that all their sheep and cattle should graze in common over all their holdings, watched over by a common herdsman.

While I was staying with this peasant, I found that many of the younger men of the village were leaving or had left for work in the towns. My host's own daughter had married a young man from the village who, however, had been trained as an engineer and had got a job in the town. The demand for skilled men in industry and the rapid industrial expansion of Russia will probably, before long, soak away into the industrial sink many of the younger generation who are now a surplus agricultural population in the village. This process, if it goes on, will tend to make the collective farms more efficient units of production than they are at present with their large amount of redundant labour.

We visited the 'House of Culture' which had been erected since I was there last. There were places to read newspapers, and a small library, a stage for plays and a display of agricultural targets which the collective farm members are asked to attain in the coming year. The farm, it was said, had produced so much corn, milk, sheep and cattle last year and now the target for this year was so much more, another twenty per cent. and more still for the year after. Across the way was the primary and secondary school. The teachers showed much pride in taking us round. Everything seemed well appointed and clean. Outside in a little glade of birch trees were some graves of soldiers who had been killed near there in the war, and a monument to perpetuate their memory and the memory of those from the village who had fallen farther afield.

This collective farm had made surprising progress in the fourteen years since I had been there, but I could not rid myself of the feeling that, though the peasants accept the collective system, it is doubtful if they have their hearts one hundred per cent. in it. In the Ukraine the peasants have had a touch of peasant proprietorship for a time between the October Revolution of 1917 and the beginning of the forced collectivization under Stalin in the early nineteen-thirties. They probably accept collectivization less readily in the Ukraine than do the peasants of North and Central Russia, where peasant proprietorship never got so much hold in this interim period. Farther to the west of the Ukraine, collectivization is even less well received, for some two hundred miles in that direction lies Poland, where collective farming has been dropped altogether in spite of the fact that there is a Communist régime there. It seems that the farther east one goes towards the borders of Asia, the more readily does collective farming seem to be accepted. I believe it will continue in Russia, but Russian agriculture is, in spite of improvements in recent years, still very backward and is likely to be a headache to the Soviet Government which wants early results in increased food as a basis for the new and rising industrial economy. Collectivization of farming may make the technical problem of efficient agriculture easier, but my impression is that it has not got over the psychological prejudice of the peasants, particularly in places like the Ukraine.

Our time in Russia was coming to an end. We boarded the night train from Kieff to the Polish frontier. In our compartment was the wife of a young German who was studying engineering in Russia. She was returning to East Germany. She had no strong reactions to life in Russia one way or the other. Possibly she thought it best, if she had any reactions, to keep them to herself. But we could conclude that, to many East Germans, Russia must be a magnet which draws them to opportunities and careers. But whether in that way the

Agriculture and the Ukrainian Village

Russian Communists can attract the mass of East Germans into their system we could not guess.

Next morning, the train was rolling along slowly over the great level plain interspersed with dykes and ditches and called the Pripet Marshes. They are no longer marshes because much of it has been drained during the last hundred years. Stubble fields where corn had grown last summer were to be seen. Here and there the ground was too low to drain well and water had lain there in the winter. Now scrub birch and willow was growing, and rough grass with willow herb and meadowsweet. Cattle were roaming here and picking up a living. This is interesting country. It is here that the Pripet river, a tributary of the Dnieper, rises in the foothills of the Carpathians and threads its way through this series of marshes eastward. It was in this country that the Eastern Slavs first began to form themselves into communities during the sixth and seventh centuries A.D., and these communities by the tenth century had consolidated themselves into the Principality of Kieff. This was the first attempt of the Russians or Eastern Slavs to create a political system based on colonies of graziers in the Carpathian foot-hills and fishermen and hunters in the Pripet Marshes. From this first attempt at state-building they went on and expanded across the great plains between the Dnieper and the Volga, mixing and marrying with the little tribes of Finnish-speaking people, fishermen and fur-hunters also, who had been there for centuries. So they founded the Russian State which became the Empire and finally the Soviet Union. It is often said—'Scratch a Russian and you find a Tartar.' That is quite untrue. The Eastern Slavs never mixed much with the Tartars, who spoke a Turkish language and came from the East. But it is true that if you scratch a Russian you may find a Finn, for these two peoples mingled in the course of centuries and many of the Russian physical features—short, stocky frame, high cheek-bones and squat noses—come from a Finnish origin. Only in Finland proper, however, did the Finns consolidate sufficiently to create a state. Elsewhere they were absorbed by the Russians. They are still, however, to be seen in their original primitive condition among the remote tribes of Northern Siberia or on the frontiers of Outer Mongolia, where they remain relatively pure and where I saw them on an expedition in 1910. For the process of mingling with the Russians is going on there now, the process that has been going on for nearly a thousand years.

In the train as we passed along towards the west, we went through the country where the Russians first tested their capacity to colonize by settling among primitive people, inter-marrying and absorbing. The Russians have, from earliest times, been peaceful colonizers, settling down with other races whom they find and fighting with them the battle against nature for a living. This has tended to make them tolerant of other races and their imperialism when it came an inter-racial one. Their hard struggle with nature has tended to level out differences, to eliminate social privilege, in other words, to create a primitive socialism. Later, of course, a caste system and serfdom came to be riveted on them, largely from outside. Their expansions, however, have always ended when they came up against better organized communities like Germans or, as they seem to be finding now in Central Asia, a culture based on a different religion.

After passing Luninetz and Baranowicze we reached Brest-Litovsk, the frontier town between Russia and Poland where the Bolsheviks in the early days of the October Revolution fought their great diplomatic fight with the Prussian Generals. Here we said good-bye to our young lady student from Moscow University, who had accompanied us for so long and helped us so greatly. Everything that we wanted to see she did her utmost to arrange for us, and when we wanted to be alone and look at things for ourselves, she left us alone. We could not have had a better guide and assistant. But it is largely a question of luck whom you get and they are not all as good as she was. And so we said good-bye, changed over to the Polish train and glided away to the west and to Germany.

CHAPTER VII

BERLIN PAST AND PRESENT

First impressions of West Berlin; Berlin humour; new architecture; reconstruction from rubble; fantastic position of West Berlin; unlikelihood of German unity in near future; previous divisions of Germany; we visit old friends in French Zone; talks over the past; memories of Rosa Luxembourg; we visit East Berlin and see sites of former great events; memories of how Republicans and Socialists were suppressed; I see former scenes of violence; lack of unity of Left; unity of militarist and impoverished middle classes created Hitlerism; we visit Communists in East Berlin and talk over the past; Communist régime milder since Stalin's death; East Berlin shops; we attend service in Lutheran church.

OUR train from Poland reached the Schlesischer Bahnhof in the early morning. This is in East Berlin. But we were able without difficulty to get across in a taxi to West Berlin. A mere showing of passports got us through the not very strict control at the Brandenburg Gate. Before long we were settled in the west of the city.

I had not recognized Berlin when I saw it on my way to Russia just after the war. All the old landmarks had gone and there was only a sea of rubble, in which well-known streets could occasionally be just recognized. The city had now been largely rebuilt, but the places where I had lived during the Weimar Republic days between 1919 and 1922 were gone, though some of the squares remained. The house where my wife and I lived after we were married in Friedenau was gone, but the Lutheran Church stood. The statues of Luther and Melanchthon had evidently been blown up by a bomb, but had been replaced. The new Melanchthon had not got the Bible in his hand, which our little daughter, aged two, had mistaken for a piece of bread and butter! The Kaiser Wilhelm Memorial Church at the end of the Kurfurstendamm was still in ruins, the tower balancing precariously on a narrow arch. Apparently it is safe, but it does not look it. The people of West Berlin, however, think more of rebuilding the utility side of their life and have not minded leaving this church as an eyesore. And meanwhile the construction of the city over the last ten years has been quite phenomenal. Blocks of flats and

Government administrative premises have sprung up, as it seemed, overnight. Several very imposing buildings have been erected such as the Technical University of Charlottenburg and the Hilton Hotel. So far there is no development of skyscrapers as in Moscow. But I could not help thinking that possibly too much is being left to private enterprise. However, the Germans have always had a great sense of discipline and I was assured that municipal planners do have some say. There must have been enormous capital investments from Federal West Germany poured into here together with considerable sums of American Marshall Aid. Berlin has been practically rebuilt, but here and there a patch of the old rubble remains. This, too, is being tackled and something was in process of building. The free enterprise of the West has certainly succeeded in creating a new life and the Berliners must have been buoyed up in their spirits in the difficult post-war years by that saving grace, their sense of humour, not unspiced with a little cynicism. There is no part of Germany where the people have such a robust common sense as in Berlin. It was so in the Kaiser's time, and the Berlin jokes about the Kaiser were endless. It was so in the Weimar Republic days, and the tragedy of that abortive régime was always accurately, if caustically, reflected in the Berlin humour of that time. And when the Nazi terror régime came, the Berliners' humanity showed itself as well in openly defying authority and being decent to Jews in public places where such an act might have had serious consequences. Now the Berliner has another butt for his humour, the Russian Communists in East Berlin. Endless tales could be told about this. Berlin never was at any time a very attractive city. It was largely built at a time when utility, not art, dominated architecture. But that has probably stimulated what the Germans call *galgenhumor* ('humour of the gallows'), just as a similar sense seems to have been stimulated among the people of Lancashire in their wet, raw climate and bleak industrial towns.

But we saw some modern architecture in a corner of the old Tiergarten. Here flats had been erected of the latest style which were clearly the ideas of some designers and architects and were very striking in their conceptions. Many eminent architects, among them the Frenchman Corbusier, have been working in Berlin. And to cap it all were two new churches, a Protestant and a Roman Catholic. One had to look hard at them to be sure that they were churches. They looked more like a pavilion for some international show or exhibition. There was clearly more artistic and original thinking and designing here than in anything that we saw in Moscow, where the new buildings were in general drab, uniform and conventional.

Coming from Russia and looking at the shops of West Berlin, it seemed as if one had come from a desert to an oasis. They were more like those of London, Paris or Rome and were bulging with every sort of consumer and durable consumer goods. The housekeeper could have all his or her wants supplied in food and household equipment. One thought at first that prices might be too high and that they were only for the rich. But the articles of clothing, footwear, household equipment and furniture were not only there in abundance and were of excellent quality, but on examination it was found that the prices were certainly no higher than in Russia and in some cases much cheaper. Of course, West Berlin being in the front line may have some special privileges and the private enterprise economy may be modified by hidden subsidies for political reasons. One rather suspects that that may be the case at least with some articles. But the general conclusion one comes to when walking along the Kurfurstendamm and the side streets is that the free economy of the West is delivering the goods as far as West Berlin is concerned.

Yet the situation of West Berlin is little short of fantastic. Here is half a city with a population of a little under two and a half million completely surrounded by the Communist-controlled land of East Germany, whose capital is the East part of Berlin with a population of a million and a quarter. The two parts of the city are there cheek-by-jowl. You can walk from one part of the city into the other generally without pass control or only a very perfunctory one. There is no control on the trams or the underground railway. Yet the Governments are quite different and the authorities hardly on speaking terms. They have each separate currency and, incidentally, the mark of West Berlin is about four times the value of the mark of East Berlin and a currency black market is, of course, flourishing. There is nothing like this state of affairs anywhere in the world, but West Berlin is a prestige counter for the West. It is, of course, a constant irritant for the Communist-controlled East Germany with its aid of Russian bayonets to bolster it up. The West Berliners are solidly anti-Communist. Though no parties are allowed to take part in elections in East Germany or East Berlin other than Communist parties, in West Berlin elections are free and Communists run candidates. At a recent general election, the Communists obtained a quite insignificant vote. This shows clearly enough what West Berliners think of Communism.

It is small wonder that various attempts have been made by Communist Russia to alter this state of affairs. The first was in 1948 when Stalin attempted to blockade and starve West Berlin. We all know how the heroic air-lift showed Stalin that nothing less than war would give him control over West Berlin. He was afraid and dropped it. In November 1958 Krushchev attempted a milder and more subtle form of the same idea. The East German Communist

Government was to be recognized by all the Powers, Russia would sign a Peace Treaty with it, the Western Powers would withdraw and Berlin become a neutral zone. With Russian troops, if not in Berlin, at least somewhere in East Germany supporting its ally, it could be guessed how long the city would remain neutral. The general election in West Berlin, with its overwhelming anti-Communist vote, was the reply to this. Ever since then, West Berliners have regarded themselves as more than ever the advance-guard of the anti-Communist front in Central Europe.

When I was received by the Oberbürgermeister Herr Brandt in Government House at Steglitz, I was shown the hall where the Parliament of West Berlin meets. The flags of all the 'Länder' of Federal West Germany were there, including those of West Berlin. They are there in anticipation of the meeting of the Federal West German Parliament which they hope will be held there soon. It has not yet met there, and with good reason, for that would certainly be too great a provocation in the present delicate situation. But the place is kept ready for that Parliament. It seems unlikely that German unity will be attained in the lifetime of our older generation and perhaps not of those either in middle life today. Russia, since she realized during the nineteen-twenties that social revolution was not going to sweep across Europe and create a chain of Soviet Republics, has been busy creating satellite states on her western borders in military alliance with her. She has never forgotten Hitler's treacherous attack on her in June 1942 and she will never allow that to happen again. East Germany is part of this chain of satellite states. It is rough justice and I find it hard to avoid the conclusion that the world has got to live with this set-up throughout the foreseeable future.

This is not the first time that Germany has been divided into two political systems. After Napoleon's victory at Jena, when Prussia lay prostrate before him, two Germanys came into existence, divided very much as at present along a line which, in part at least, follows the river Elbe or at least the Elbe basin. To the west was the Confederation of the Rhine with its free institutions created by the French Republic, though modified by Napoleon's military system. To the east of this border-line lay another Germany under the King of Prussia with junkers' estates and peasant serfdom. That Germany lasted some years and ended with the defeat of Napoleon. We have something like it now in twentieth-century surroundings. But the Soviet régime in Russia is more firmly based than Napoleon ever was. So this partition of Germany set up by Russia with the Western Allies' tacit agreement after the war is likely to be much more lasting. Under the present arrangements, West Germany has civic freedom and individual liberty very much as Napoleon's Confederation of the

Rhine had. East Germany has now got rid of the junkers' estates and all relics of feudalism, but it has the modern equivalent of the Prussian system in the dictatorship, not of landlords, but of an intellectual communist oligarchy.

We had not been long in West Berlin before we decided to try and find some friends whom we remembered from the far-off days in the early nineteen-twenties, when forty years ago I was 'covering' the Weimar Republic for the *Daily Herald*. After some enquiry, we traced a man and his wife living in the French Zone. She had been a great friend of my wife. Together they had worked in the Dynamo works of Siemens-Schukert and together they had been members of the youth movement of the German Social Democratic Party. We found them in a rather grim part of Berlin with long streets of drab, grey houses, many of them still showing signs of war damage. They lived half-way up a bleak staircase in a comfortable little flat and he had a job in a Government department of West Berlin. They were overjoyed to see us and we spent the evening telling each other of our adventures in the intervening years since we had first met after the First World War in Berlin and in the early days of the Weimar Republic. Their story was typical of many of the Socialist working class during those years of *Sturm und Drang*, of stress and struggle. Like many of the workers of Western and Central Europe, they had enthusiastically acclaimed the fall of the Tsarist autocracy of Russia. Light was coming from the East while all around were the jack-boots of the East Prussian militarists, the junker-ridden régime of Wilhelm Hohenzollern and the armament kings of Westphalia. That enthusiasm did not fade, when the Kerensky régime in Russia was succeeded by the Bolshevik Revolution and the Communist dictatorship. They had both joined the Communist Party and, when I first met them, he had some job on the Party's central newspaper. They took part in demonstrations, carried banners, assisted strikes and addressed meetings. Russia must be helped, they said, against the German militarists and the French and British imperialists who were trying to suppress the Revolution. I was reporting for my paper all that was going on in Germany at that time and remembered coming across them from time to time. I had meanwhile married her friend, and then she and my wife did not see each other so often, but remained friends.

Meanwhile the revolution in Germany went a different way to that of Russia. The National Assembly sat in Weimar, the Republic was founded and peace was made with the Western Powers. Then the Communist Party had to face the fact that the middle classes in Germany were stronger than in Russia, while the working classes were divided between revolutionaries and reformists, Communists and Social-democrats. Our two friends were at the parting of the ways. The Communist Party of Germany was divided and it was felt that the inevitable must be faced, since the revolutionary wave in Europe was receding. So many thought they must go slow until some new international crisis would come and a new crisis would arise. Lenin had meanwhile died and that brilliant Polish Communist and colleague of Karl Liebknecht, Rosa Luxembourg, had been murdered in January 1919. She had from the beginning opposed Lenin's theory that the Communist Party must dominate all parties and dictate its will to the working classes.[1] Though ready to use a dictatorship over the middle and propertied classes, she was not prepared to see it dominate over the other working-class parties. The Russian Communist Party moreover, she said, must not give orders to the other parties. There must be common consultation and mutual respect. But she was murdered by agents of the military reaction before she could take the lead of the Communists in Germany. Meanwhile, many Communists began to drop out or take a line of their own, for they would not accept Russian domination. The next time I had seen our host and his wife was in 1922, when he was editing a Communist paper in South Germany. I was investigating certain problems of the French occupation of the Rhineland and I met them in the more congenial atmosphere of a small German provincial town, where the group of Communists, far removed from Moscow, were adopting a much milder form of their Party's philosophy. But things were beginning to deteriorate. The extreme Right in Germany was coming back to power and everything ended in Hitler a few years later.

When Hitler came to power they were arrested because they were Communists and brought before the so-called People's Tribunals. They described to us how they had played off their judges by showing that they had resisted the attempts of the Russian Communists to dominate the Communists of Germany. This seems to have confounded Hitler's legal people and they were in due course released and managed to get out into France. Here they found a more congenial atmosphere and lived there till the war. But after France fell it required all their ingenuity then to keep out of the clutches of the Nazis, who wanted to seize them and bring them back to Germany to stand trial for 'anti-German' activities. How they succeeded was incredible, for the Vichy régime was prepared to hand them over. However, they did manage to get decisions to extradite them put off till the Normandy invasion and the break-up of the Hitler régime. Their story was typical of many in those years. The German working classes had a healthy suspicion of things Russian. What might do for

[1] See Chapter II, p. 32.

Russia with her history and background would not necessarily do for Germany with her history and background. Orderliness and planned building-up had more attraction to many German workers than the Nihilist theory of sweeping everything away and building-up on completely clear ground. Tsarist methods might be seen in the Bolsheviks and some German workers wanted neither. Our two friends were of this sort. This point of view, moreover, was particularly strong in Berlin, where the people are notoriously hard-headed, independent-minded and tough. I had remembered forty years ago hearing that sort of thing said about Russian Communism by people who were good working class socialists. These then were the sort of people who still inhabit West Berlin and who form a good part of the working-class population of that sturdy city. We were pleased that we had been able to seek out these old friends, whom we had remembered in those far-off days and who had fought in the struggles of those years. They were, like us, of course older and with greying hairs, but their views had not changed with the passage of time. They wanted a Social Democratic Germany. They had helped to defeat Hitler and, as before, they had their faces directed against Moscow's attempts to impose their system on Germany.

We spent a good part of several days exploring East Berlin, entering by the Brandenburg Gate. Here we saw that many landmarks had completely disappeared, while others had been so altered as to be hardly recognizable. For instance, just inside the 'frontier' was the site of the former Adlon Hotel, the centre of the most fashionable society of Berlin, of Hohenzollern and Weimar Republic days. I used to go there to meet fellow-journalists and to seek interviews. It has vanished, and in its place is a small hostel. The old French Embassy was also gone, the Wilhelmstrasse a shadow of its former self and the old Foreign Office was non-existent. The limes of Unter den Linden were about the only things that seemed unaltered. The Russian Embassy, of course, was much enlarged and the most imposing building in the whole area. At the top of Unter den Linden nothing was recognizable except the cathedral, which had been badly damaged in the bombardment and was not restored. It seemed to be falling into decay. The great museum with its wonderful collections from classical Greece and Rome was standing, but it was not open and it appeared to have nothing in it. Where the Kaiser's Palace stood is an open space and a sports ground for exhibitions and demonstrations. Communist slogans were displayed everywhere on banners or painted on hoardings. All this on the site of where Hohenzollern majesty once ruled! Indeed poetic justice!

And yet I remember that on this spot I had witnessed forty years ago in 1919 many stirring events and also several grim ones. The

Democratic Republic was struggling for life on the ruins of Hohenzollern militarism. On the steps of the cathedral I had seen many prominent figures of those days addressing vast crowds of Berliners on May Day. Here I remembered seeing Ebert, later President of the Republic, then Scheidemann, later Prime Minister, address great crowds. I remember them stressing the need for law and order and the observance of constitutional methods. The people, they said, must trust the parliamentary democracy that was being set up by the Republic. I then remember Heinrich Ströbel, one of the Social-democrat leaders. He was not so complacent as Ebert and Scheidemann, for he warned the workers of Berlin that the military leaders of Hohenzollern Germany were still there and ready to suppress the Republic. 'These generals', he said, 'may be good soldiers, but they are bad politicians.'

On another spot near the cathedral I saw a large meeting addressed by Communist speakers. They warned, like some of the Social-democrats, of the danger from the Right, but they did not leave it at that. They called for the arming of the factory workers to resist the reaction. At another place I remember having seen Independent Socialist speakers. They took an intermediate position between Ebert and Scheidemann on the one hand and the Communists on the other and were more like the Left-wing Social-democrats of the type of Ströbel. They, too, warned against the militarists, but had no advice on how to stop them. Some were eloquent speakers. There was Rudolph Breitscheid, a fine orator, who was later handed over by the Vichy French to the Gestapo and done to death after the fall of France. What he feared came only too true. His speech was the dirge predicting his own fate and the fate of many other good German progressives and socialists. Then there was Georg Ledebour, one of the bravest fighters for German freedom and democracy. He had just been acquitted of a charge of conspiracy which had been trumped up against him. He received a great ovation. He went on fighting to the end, but when all was lost and Hitler came to power, he managed to get into Switzerland and died in his bed there. My wife visited him just before the end. Not far away from this spot was a street along the River Spree, where lived Paul Dreyfus, who acted for me in getting information for my despatches to the *Daily Herald*. He was a colleague of that great Social-democrat, Edward Bernstein, who recommended him to me. Here was a quiet, painstaking man, seeking no publicity, hiding his light under a bushel, but full of native wisdom and seeing clearly the main issues in the jungle of contemporary German politics. I found him invaluable. He was always warning that the Prussian military caste, the East Elbian junkers and the big industrialists were only driven underground by the defeat in the

7 Collective Farm in Ukraine—cattle shed

Collective Farm in Ukraine—our host and family with Mrs Price and guide

Soviet Weekly

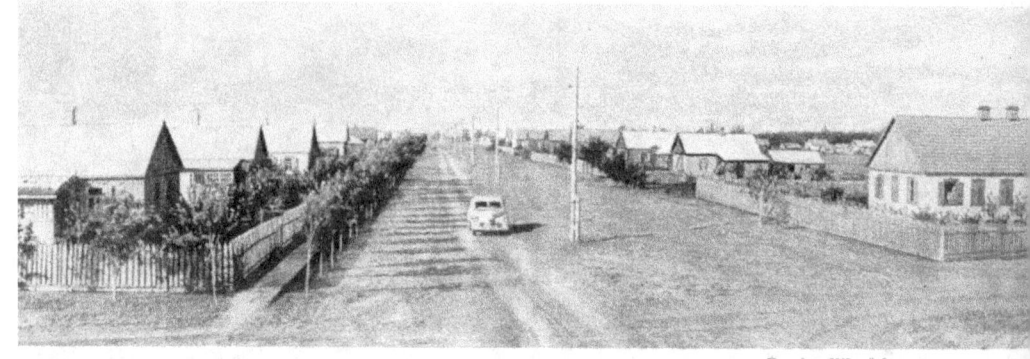

8 Collective Farm in village in North Russia

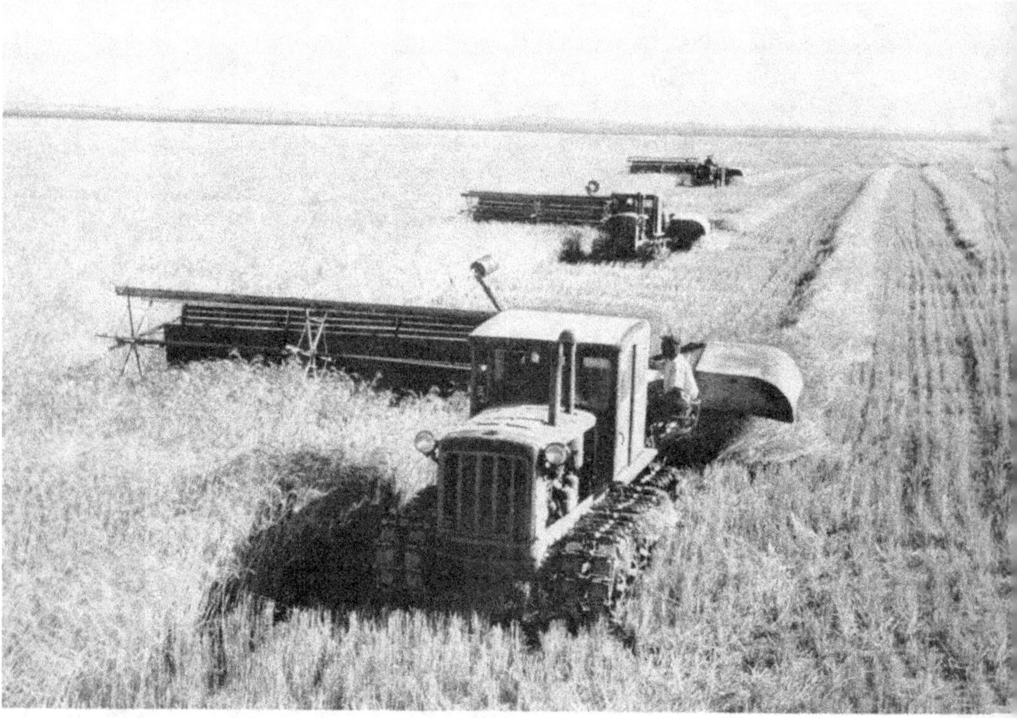

Soviet Weekly

Collective Farm in Kazakistan—modern harvesting

World War. The Allies, he said, made a great mistake in not giving support to the constitutional Republican Left in Germany. The Right would come back, he said, possibly in a worse form than before. He said this in 1919. Fourteen years later Hitler was in power and his words were proved only too true. He died in an internment camp in Vichy France in 1940. At least he was not handed over to the Gestapo. I often feel that the tragedy of the German progressives in those days was enough to make an angel weep.

To the north of the spot where the Kaiser's Palace once stood was another open space. Here was once the Marstall or royal stables connected with the Palace. I remember that in that building some sailors of the German Navy from Kiel were established with machine-guns and rifles. They had refused to give up their arms to the Coalition Government of Social-democrats and the Catholic Party (Zentrum) without some guarantee of their safety and the disarming also of Right Wing formations and members of the Prussian Officers' Corps who were in Berlin at the time. A detachment of troops from the still not yet disbanded Imperial Army under Prussian officers had carried the Marstall by assault and had murdered every man of the Marines. Who was responsible for this was never established, but it was a clear indication that the Republican Coalition had not got the situation in hand. I had been in the Marstall to interview the Marines and only just got out in time. I went there after the massacre and I shall not forget it. That and the murder of Karl Liebknecht and Rosa Luxembourg were the first signals of the advancing reaction which ultimately wrecked the Democratic Republic.

One of the things that struck me most in Germany during these days was the fact that the Socialist and Republican Left were hopelessly divided and could not act together against the Right. German democracy was still very young and had little experience. Curiously enough, the Left in Russia seemed in these days to have had more cohesion. Consequently the October Revolution succeeded and one party, the Bolsheviks, after a great struggle did succeed in holding on and founding the Soviet Union. In Germany, the Left was unable to show enough cohesion, while the Hohenzollern militarists were sufficiently united to attract other elements of society. The middle classes, impoverished by inflation, had formed a new Right which ultimately took on a barbarous form and swept all before it in Hitler.

Another thing that struck me at that time was the fact that complete ruthlessness paid dividends. Karl Liebknecht and Rosa Luxembourg were the first victims of a systematic campaign of assassination. Within a short time of their deaths, however, Hugo

Haase was shot on the steps of the Reichstag. Then Kurt Eisner, the Bavarian Socialist Prime Minister, was murdered on the steps of the Diet in Munich. There followed most of the Communist leaders. Then came the turn of the Catholic leaders and Conservative Republicans and Erzberger was assassinated. Finally, it was the turn of the millionaire capitalist, Walter Rathenau, because he was a Jew. He was done to death near his home in Berlin. Not one of these murderers was brought to justice, except the last one, and he, after he had escaped, was killed in a running fight in Central Germany. Some of the others who were caught were tried, but acquitted on the grounds that they had acted under 'patriotic motives'. Others were imprisoned, but escaped within a few weeks and got out of Germany. They were spirited across the frontier into Hungary, where the Fascist régime of Admiral Horthy ruled. Public opinion in Germany then seemed quite unmoved by all this. Protests were only raised in the Socialist and Communist press and a few Liberal papers like the *Berliner Tageblatt* and the *Vossische Zeitung*. It appeared that after defeat in the First World War public morale had sunk to such a low ebb that only political gangsterdom could make any impression or obtain authority.

I often used to think during these times that the victorious Allies were only laying up trouble for themselves in not intervening in the internal affairs of Germany. There was complete anarchy there in 1919 and till about 1925. Any gangster, sufficiently ruthless, could get control and run the country. The Liberals and Progressives in Germany, who were there and struggling, were suppressed or had to flee abroad. The same thing happened then as happened after 1848 when Bismark and the King of Prussia suppressed the Frankfurt National Assembly and all Germans with Liberal ideas had to flee abroad or pine in prisons for years. Some of these Germans helped Lincoln to free the slaves in America, but they were lost to Germany. The Versailles Treaty which ended the First World War imposed heavy reparations on Germany which only increased the chaos but left the internal politics of Germany uncontrolled. The result was in the end Hitler and the Second World War. At the end of this war, however, the right thing was done. Germany was made to surrender unconditionally and the result was that the budding German democracy was not torn off and destroyed but allowed to develop. Nazis were hunted out and the worst put under lock and key. If that had happened after the First World War, history might have been different. These thoughts came to me after visiting the sites where I had seen the Weimar Republic struggling after the First World War forty years ago.

One of the more interesting experiences in East Berlin was a visit which we paid to another married couple who were friends of my wife and myself in the early days of the Weimar Republic. They were both Communists, and still are. They took part in the great struggle of the early nineteen-twenties to prevent the military reaction from getting control of Germany again. They fought with Liebknecht and Luxembourg and, after they were murdered, with their less well-known successors. We had not seen them since Hitler came to power and were interested to know what had happened to them in the meantime. The friends we had visited in the French Zone a few days before were typical of those who had broken with the Communists, realizing how unsuitable their system was for Germany. But here were two Communists who had only broken with the system during the worst of the Stalin terror and had since his death gone back and been re-admitted. They were, if one can use the phrase, moderate and tolerant Communists. They are typical of a number of German workers who were originally attracted to the Russian Revolution when it was struggling to establish itself, but who retained their independent judgment, while being at the same time convinced that Communist methods were the only ones to prevent Germany from falling again a victim to the Fascists.

We went to the outskirts of East Berlin bordering on the Brandenburg Forest and found them in a comfortable little bungalow. The story they told us was as follows. With the coming of Hitler, they went underground and worked in the illegal anti-Fascist organizations. Things got too hot for them and they had to leave and got into France. The war broke out and the collapse of France made their position desperate. After hair's-breadth escapes they got across the Pyrenees into Spain. They separated, disguised themselves and lived in Spain for a while. Finally they got taken over separately as refugees by an American organization and reached the United States, where they met again. When the war ended they returned to Germany and worked for the Communists in East Berlin. But again things got too hot, this time from another quarter. Stalin was starting his treason trials and purges and was ordering the Communist Parties in various parts of the world, including Germany, to obey orders from Moscow without question. They objected that the Communist Party of Germany should be a vehicle for Russian instructions. They held to the views of the Communist leader, Rosa Luxembourg, that the dictatorship of the working class should not degenerate into the dictatorship of the Communist Party, and least of all of the Russian Communist Party, over the working class. So they protested and were thrown out of the Party. But they were not molested, although they lost their jobs and found it hard to get others. They stuck it out, however, till Stalin died, when the atmosphere improved and they were allowed back into the Party again. He was given a job of lecturer on history in a Marxist Institute in East Berlin. Here he was able to exercise his independent judgment up to a point and to treat past events objectively. We put many questions to him and his wife over supper and formed the impression that since the Krushchev régime there had been greater toleration than under Stalin of individual views among Communists. The atmosphere is more liberal than it was, but in East Germany there is still less freedom to express independent opinions than there is today in Russia.

We spent a little time looking round the shops of East Berlin. The contrast with West Berlin was very striking and one might be in Russia again. There were fewer articles for sale and, compared with the prices in West Berlin and having regard to the value of the East German mark, the prices were dearer. Here in the same city were two economic worlds. Food was abundant and cheap as in Russia, but there was shortage and inferior quality in consumer goods and household utensils. It seems that much of East Germany's industrial effort is going to supply capital goods for Russia.

Our last impression of East Berlin was on a Sunday, when we decided to go to the Lutheran service in the Marienkirche, the old Protestant church in the centre of the city, but in the Russian Zone. It was here that Bishop Dibelius sometimes preached, but one of his colleagues took the service that Sunday. Taking our seats in the centre of the church, we watched the congregation arrive. To our surprise, we saw the church fill up with a large number of quite young people of both sexes. There was an intense earnestness in their faces which indicated defiance of the régime under which they were living. Here undoubtedly were to be seen that element of the anti-Communists in East Berlin who remain loyal to the old Lutheran church. In the Lutheran service there is no procession of the Pastor and the choir. The latter were in the gallery containing the organ and the Pastor suddenly appeared from nowhere and the service began. Hymns alternated with prayers and psalms, all said and sung with great fervour. Much of the music seemed to be from old Lutheran chants. The Pastor himself had a heavy frame, looked rugged and tough with a face like a granite quarry. He was a perfect edition of a latter-day Luther and his sermons fitted the tradition and the occasion. Do not compromise with Evil, he said. Fight the good fight. You are the Elect of God, chosen to resist the wrong. A firm stronghold is our God. His sermon contained the essence of Lutheran Protestantism. It was an appeal for action. Salvation comes through works. Belief and creeds come second. And the work to be done is the struggle with Evil. Of course, the setting for this sort of religious attitude is perfect, when you are living under a Communist régime. But in the days of the Hohenzollerns it was different. The Lutheran Church then supported the establishment. The evil ones were the Socialists. But I at least am inclined to forgive the past in view of the courageous attitude of the Lutheran Church in East Germany today. Some may go too far now. Bishop Dibelius himself has often said that good Lutherans must not obey the laws of the Communist State. In this he has not followed the advice of his Master who would 'Render to Caesar the things that are Caesar's.'

CHAPTER VIII

A VISIT TO EAST GERMANY

How we got a permit to go; thoughts on Potsdam as we passed it in the train; East German trains; signs of much industrial activity; arrival in Halberstadt; we visit a village; we meet and talk with peasants; threats of forced collective farming; peasant reactions; comparison between land-holding systems in Germany, Poland and Russia; we visit the village church; we return to Halberstadt; reflection on the old town walls; we visit scenes of my wife's childhood; shabbiness of everything; Communist propaganda; destruction of part of town by Allied bombers in war; friendly reception by the people we meet; no resentment about wartime bombing; great resentment at Communist régime; we visit the old cathedral; the two souls of old Germany; the partition of Germany today; will process of liberalization affect Communism in East Germany as it has in Poland and to some extent in Russia?

IT required a few days to get a permit to enter the territory of the East German Republic and several trips from West to East Berlin, where passes could be obtained, were first necessary. We were told by people in West Berlin that the task was hopeless and that, unless we were a member of some organization connected with the Communists or held some public position in the West which might be subject to Communist influence or be affected by propaganda, there was no chance for us as private individuals. As I had just ceased to be an MP, and our only excuse that we wanted to see my wife's birthplace, we had to approach the authorities as very ordinary people with no pull of any kind. However, it did seem that the authorities were not so inflexible as we were told in West Berlin that they would be.

The East Berlin police authorities to whom we had to go were polite, but not speedy in their activities. They improved the shining hour by informing us that it would take much less time if only the Western Powers would recognize the East German Republic. But we got our permission to go to Halberstadt all right and to spend two nights there if we wished. Then we had to get the rail tickets and the East German currency, and all that took time. I compared this with the days when I lived in Germany under the Weimar Republic and what I remembered of Hohenzollern days. It seemed inconceivable that so mighty an Empire should now be partitioned like a Balkan state. In the old days I had just gone to the Potsdamer Bahnhof and bought myself a ticket for Halberstadt and was there in a few hours. Today I might be crossing the frontier into Afghanistan or Tibet. This only shows on what shallow foundations the Hohenzollern Empire and its successor, the Weimar Republic, had stood In Frederick the Great's day, during one of his bad periods, the hooves of Cossack horses had been heard in the streets of Berlin, but that soon passed. Today the set-up seems as if it is going to be of long standing.

In due course we boarded a train at the Schlesischer Bahnhof bound for the west part of East Germany. We followed a circuitous route to avoid the Western Allies' Zone in Berlin. It took us about an hour to cover what formerly took ten minutes from Central Berlin to Potsdam in a fast train. We crawled along over loop lines and junctions and at last reached Potsdam. Outside the station our passes were carefully examined and some had their baggage looked at too, but we had virtually nothing with us. I longed to get out and have a look at Potsdam, which I had known so well in former days, visit the tomb of Frederick the Great and hear the chimes of the garrison church clock ringing the old Lutheran hymn 'Praise to the Lord, the Almighty, the King of Creation'. The last time I had been there the church was a shell and the old clock silent. The tomb of the Great Prussian king was open and his remains had been sent to Central Germany. I do not know what has happened to them since, but the garrison church, from what I could see from the train, seemed to have been restored. So the train passed on through the orchards of Werder into the forests, swamps and lakes to the east of old Brandenburg.

The train reminded us of what we had seen and experienced in Russia. Instead of the tidiness and cleanliness that generally characterize things German, there was messiness, dusty compartments, doors that jammed and closets which were anything but savoury. Indeed, the trains we were in in Russia were much better than those in East Germany. There seemed to be a brisk business going on and at various stations we passed freight trains bound eastwards and laden with agricultural machinery and engineering goods of all kinds. East Germany seemed to be supplying industrial goods and machinery for Russia. We had seen an example of this in Moscow when we visited their textile factory and found much of its modern machinery made in East Germany. Magdeburg, that unattractive town on the River Elbe, was a hive of activity and the centre evidently of considerable traffic.

We arrived at Halberstadt and decided to go out to a village a few miles from the old town, where my wife's mother was born. We found a car with a driver at the station who was willing to take us there. It was a typical village of Central Germany. Old red-brick and half-timbered houses were nestling round a church. There were narrow streets, yards where cattle were housed and land implements kept. There was picturesque confusion, but the land round the village was carefully cultivated. It was autumn, corn crops had been harvested and the land was being prepared for autumn sowing. We went to the house of the Lutheran Pastor. He was away, but his wife was at home. When she heard that we were British, her face shone with pleasure. She could not believe that English people should want to come to an unimportant little village like this. We explained that we were interested to get some information about my wife's mother and her forebears. She went off and got the district nurse, who knew some old people who might remember my wife's mother or had heard about her. Together we went round the village and entered several peasant houses and talked with the people. We were only partially successful in getting the information we sought, and we found one old man who just remembered my wife's mother but knew little else. It was a question of consulting the parish registers, and they were not complete. Meanwhile, we became aware of the fact that something was seriously worrying the peasants of this village. Without our asking, they informed us that the Communist authorities had ordered a meeting in the village at which the peasants were told that they must turn their individual holdings into a collective farm. Indeed, preparations for this had already taken place and a number of peasants had had their land requisitioned and were told that they must work it in common with their neighbours. Not much in this respect, however, seems to have been done in practice. There were no depots for communally-used implements, there was no central administrative bureau, no common cattle-sheds, like we had seen in the collective farm we had visited in the Ukraine. Nor were individual holdings proposed, as in the Ukraine, which the peasants could work in addition to working on the collective farm. It seemed as if the whole village had been placed upon a Procrustean bed by some Communist administrators in the nearest town and for the moment left. But everyone realized that before long more drastic measures would be adopted. The whole village set-up and type of farming seemed for the moment to be going on as it had for centuries past, individual holdings with the equipment of each attached to the peasant's house, building and yard. But we could see a look of bewilderment on the faces of the peasants we met. They were silent and obviously distressed by what was being threatened to them.

This alien power from above had suddenly descended on the village and was trying to uproot the customs and traditions of generations. Central Germany is the country of small farmers who never knew large landlords and have not since the Middle Ages been subject to feudal lords. It is quite unlike Germany east of the River Elbe with its landless peasants and junkers' estates now, of course, largely converted into State farms and 'collectives'. Something can be said for collective farming there. It had been imposed by the Russians on the Polish peasants after the Second World War, but the successful Polish Revolt in the autumn of 1956 had resulted in the suppression of collective farming in Poland under the Gomulka régime. Large tracts of Poland are like Germany east of the Elbe. But it has been dropped in Poland, where conditions are not so unsuitable for collective farming, because the peasants did not want it, went slow and did not produce the food. Yet this farming system is being forced on the Central German peasants, who have a longer tradition of individual farming even than Poland or in fact anywhere else in Central or Eastern Europe. The tradition of collective farming was completely foreign to this part of Germany. We realized what was going to happen and instinctively felt, as we walked about those narrow streets and talked to these quiet, hardy and weather-beaten German peasants, that, troubled though they were, there was a determination about them quite as strong as among the Polish peasants who, in 1956, had made collectivization of farming in Poland unworkable.

Before we left the village, the Pastor's wife took us round the little church. It was perched up on a mound overlooking the village and its old stones had weathered the storms of centuries. Judging by its age, it may have been a Catholic church before the Reformation and Luther or his assistants may have preached there once. The Pastor's wife told us that her husband relied entirely on voluntary contributions from the village for his support and for the maintenance of the church. The roof needed repairing and there were holes in it. The money was there, but they could not get permission from the authorities to buy building material. Apparently, though it was fifteen years since the war and building material was abundant and free in West Germany, this was not the case in the East German Republic.

We left the village and drove back in our car through tidy farm lands and along a road lined with trees to Halberstadt. We entered the town and drove along the relics of the old mediaeval wall. This wall must have been standing and more or less whole when a great-uncle of mine on my mother's side, Mark Philips, the first MP for Manchester in the Reform Parliament of 1832, came to Halberstadt in 1828. He travelled in a horse and carriage and was making his way across Germany to Russia, where he was hoping to do business, for he was a Manchester cotton merchant. He described in his diary how he reached Halberstadt late one night in May and found the town gate closed. In order to get in, his postillion blew 'several blasts on the horn to rouse the porter to open the gates'. Halberstadt must then have been contained within these mediaeval walls. Probably it had not more inhabitants then than it had in the Middle Ages, because the country had not yet recovered from the devastation of the Thirty Years War. Today, the town is well outside those crumbling heaps of stone which were once the walls and are now covered by bramble and elder and forgotten by everyone. The graveyard where some of my wife's forebears, including her mother, were buried lies outside what was once those walls. Industrial growth during the nineteenth century had caused all these Central German cities and towns to burst their mediaeval bonds. Halberstadt was no exception.

We went straight to the part of the old city east of the cathedral, which is perched up on a small hill. The old half-timbered houses were all there and the narrow streets just as they were when my wife was a child and as I remembered them when, with her, I came to visit the place after we were married. But the houses looked shabby and neglected now, so unlike the usual German tidiness. There had been no paint on them for years, and very little, if any, repairs. But the people were going quietly about their business as usual. The only thing one noticed was that there were frequent placards and posters proclaiming the wonders of the Soviet régime of East Germany and an occasional loudspeaker announcing the same. But no one seemed to take the slightest notice and went on with their work or whatever they were doing. We went to look at schools which my wife had attended as a child, to the little house where she had lived as an orphan with an old woman after her mother had died. We looked at the old prison and then the square outside the town hall where the 'Uhlans' or cavalry regiment, stationed in Halberstadt, paraded on important occasions. We looked for the old town hall, once a lovely old place. It was gone and heaps of rubble were all that remained. The old market-hall, mediaeval and half-timbered, was gone too. West and north-west of the cathedral we looked out over many acres of stone and brick heaps where willow-herb and nettle were now growing. Somewhere here had been a 'Junker' works making aircraft during the war.

This may have been in part the reason for the calamity that overwhelmed Halberstadt. But there was something more to it than that. According to the information given to us by people whom we met and also from German press-cuttings of events at the end of the war, we ascertained that on April 7, 1945, when German resistance was virtually at an end and the Allied armies were converging from the east and west, heavy American bombers appeared over the town and in half an hour the whole place west and north-west of the cathedral was a heap of smoking ruins. Two thousand people were buried alive and nine thousand buildings were destroyed. I felt a deep sense of shame when I looked on the scene of devastation. It is impossible to conceive that, at that stage of the war, such an action was warranted either militarily or politically.

We walked half-dazed about that part of the town we had once known. One of the old churches which we passed, the St Martin's, was a shell, but the old Roland, a stone statue of a mythical figure supposed to guard the town, had been built into the wall to preserve it for the future after it had collapsed in the old market-place. My wife had particular feelings for this church, for over the entrance there used to be a carved figure of St Martin on a horse in the process of cutting his cloak in two with his sword to give one half to a naked beggar suffering from cold. It had made a great impression on her childish mind.

Needless to say, all this was very distressing to us. My wife's home and where she went to school had been preserved. But where she had run errands to shops, bought little sweets and played with other children was a scene of devastation. My wife wept and I, too, who knew it as it was some forty years ago, went about for the rest of the day with a lump in my throat.

We consoled ourselves, however, by looking at the old cathedral which, by the mercy of God, had escaped any very serious damage. We rang the bell at the house of one of the officials corresponding in the Lutheran Church to our cathedral canons. A lady came out and, when she heard we were English, her face beamed and she welcomed us. She fetched the custodian, a delightful man, who had great pride in showing us the church treasure, which had been re-collected and had only recently been opened to the public. The cathedral had suffered some damage, but money had been found by the Lutheran authorities of the diocese, and apparently the building materials were forthcoming and the place was now in good order. One must acknowledge that the Communist régime had at least raised no objection to procuring the building material for this purpose. Soon after, we went into a bookshop and stationer's to get some books and postcards and got into conversation with the owner of the shop. Again, when he heard that we were British, he could not do enough for us. He told us that his business had been municipalized but that he was allowed to take so much of the profits of the business for himself, while the rest had to go to the municipal treasury. It looked like a fifty per cent. income tax.

Everywhere we went, we saw no signs of Communist activity in the sense that there seemed to be no Communist Party premises in a prominent place and no sign of the activity of Communist youth, as you see all over Russia. There were, of course, local authority offices and there must have been a local Soviet, consisting of persons nominated by Communist authorities in Berlin. But one saw practically nothing of them. One heard all the time raucous voices on loudspeakers repeating Communist slogans and saw the Marxists posters and placards. But people behaved as if they did not exist. Yet, of course, all the political and economic power rested with a small coterie of Communist officials in Halberstadt. That they were hated we saw on every hand. The shopkeeper from whom we bought a few things actually gave us others and did not want us to pay because he wanted to show his pleasure that we had come to Halberstadt. He treated us as if we had come from another world, a happier world than the one he lived in. Thus the driver who drove us out to the village, the man that showed us round the cathedral, the people where we had lunch and others all seemed to forget that we were citizens of a country in alliance with another country whose air-force had half-destroyed their town. That did not seem to concern them in the least. All that they saw was that we were citizens of a free country, that we had come to visit them and they wanted us to know that the régime they had to live under was not to their liking, for it consisted of a small clique of people who ruled them on orders from East Berlin. They said this openly to us and did not mince words either, nor seemed to be afraid of being overheard. Who caused the destruction of the war was a thing of the past. It was what had come after that worried them. We may have destroyed some of their bodies in the air bombardment. But the power over them now destroyed the soul. We collected these impressions which, from all we heard, were typical of the provinces of Central Germany in the Russian Zone and, having done this, we went back to West Berlin and then home.

The old Germany that I once remembered was a united country under a strong central government with the Provinces or 'Länder' and their local governments. The people had their culture, literature, art and music for which Germany had become famous. Her political institutions were, on paper at least, similar to those of the rest of Western Europe with parliament, municipal and local councils, elected democratically. In that respect it had one foot in the West. But in another respect it had one foot in the East. The franchise of

Prussia was so weighted as to give virtual monopoly of political power to the landlords, at least in that part of Germany east of the Elbe. The Kaiser and the Berlin Government had almost complete power over foreign policy, army and navy. In the Weimar Republic democratic power which had been acquired during the revolution at the end of the First World War slowly slipped away in the years that followed. Self-appointed thugs and demagogues used the inflation and post-war chaos to attract the ruined middle classes and set up a barbarous dictatorship. Germany, in fact, was only half Western. That part of Germany ruled by Prussia had characteristics of autocratic Russia in its makeup, and this came out in times of strain. Germany was in Hohenzollern days and in the days of the Weimar Republic a buffer state between the democratic countries of the Mediterranean and Atlantic seaboard of Europe and the autocratic power of the Eurasian inner continent which had always been ruled by dictators, because only in that way could the continent be held politically together. The Germany of those days contained both those elements in its makeup.

After the Second World War, that Germany disappeared, but again the country could not become a unity and was partitioned afresh. This time the partition was more visible because it was geographical. Western Germany is now quite definitely democratic in the Western sense and has joined its fate with the countries of Western Europe. It is most important, therefore, that the peoples of France and Britain should do all they can to keep this part of Germany with them and cease to regard them as pariahs and thereby drive them back to the East once more. For Eastern Germany is now more autocratically governed than ever before and more so even than in Russia itself today. The buffer state of old Germany has gone. Instead of a state with two faces, there are two states with one face each, and very different and antagonistic faces. The only hope that a clash will not come is that in Russia the process of liberalizing Communism which is taking place slowly, and which I have noted in the earlier chapters of this book, will come also to Germany, as it did to Poland in 1956.

CHAPTER IX

A WOMAN'S IMPRESSIONS OF RUSSIA AND A VISIT TO FORMER CHILDHOOD SCENES IN GERMANY

By Mrs E. PRICE

MY first experience with Russia came at the end of the First World War when I took a job at the Russian Embassy in Berlin. It was just after the Revolution and I was twenty-three. Being a German, I had lived through the blockade, taken part in the General Strike in January 1918, which was to end all wars, had taken part in revolutionary marches in Unter den Linden and seen at first hand how the police behaved towards the workers. On one occasion I had to run from one of the pursuing policemen in blue uniform, complete with picklehelmet and sabre. I was then in fact a convinced Communist.

My job at the Russian Embassy was of the simplest and took place in the reader's room, where I met the wife of Rudolf Breitscheid, who himself was the idol of every young girl in the Socialist Movement. I was filled with great enthusiasm and I was always at the door early in the morning, long before I had to be. I was young and I believed in the World Revolution. I met members of the Embassy whom I would otherwise never have met. Some of them did not strike me as men of the earth with strong arms and heavy fists, but were, very likely, intellectuals who had belonged to that group of liberty-loving Russians who had joined the Bolshevik Party and who were, in years to come, ruthlessly weeded out by their own leaders. Uncritically I believed everything they said. I took part in every kind of public demonstration to express my belief in World Revolution. The brutal murder of Rosa Luxembourg and Karl Liebknecht in January 1919 deepened my belief. The terrible and devastating inflation, which then followed, and immensely increased the power of Hugo Stinnes and men like him, seemed to show inevitably that Russia was right. The Revolution never seemed anything terrible, but rather an outcome of conditions as they existed.

My reactions were entirely emotional, and if they are laughed at today, I do not mind. My knowledge was scant, but my feelings were of the deepest, and as far as my principles are concerned they have never changed. I say that because I wish to compare this attitude on principles with other things I later discovered, which changed my attitude to the leaders of Russian Communism. But originally everything that came from Russia was right and there was no doubt in my mind. And this was still so at the end of the Second World War, before that rush of books was published in which the less fortunate members of the Communist Party of Germany, who had been imprisoned by the Russians, described their unbelievable experiences.

It was at the very end of the last war and on V.E. Day that I got into dispute with two men who certainly did not share my belief. I was travelling from London to Gloucester and shared the compartment with an American officer, an Anglo-Indian, a very prim elderly lady and another very young American officer. A misunderstanding arose over a remark by the middle-aged officer about 'that wonderful country', by which he meant his own country, and I was stupid enough to think that he meant Russia. I took it naïvely for granted that everyone felt grateful to the Russian people for having fought such a splendid fight against Hitler's army. My mistake made him indignant and provoked me to a strong defence of Russia. The Anglo-Indian joined forces with the officer and they both became very aggressive and jumped from the general to the particular and attacked every well-known British socialist they could think of. The prim old lady shrank visibly at my un-ladylike behaviour and the young officer was obviously glad to be able to make his exit at the next halt. When the older man offered me a cigarette, I replied that I would choke on one that came from his country. An awful silence followed and lasted for an hour, when the officer looked at me with a smile and asked—'hayeh?' It broke the ice, and when he left the compartment we took a civil leave of each other.

I tell this story because up till then, and for a while even after that, I never felt any doubt about anything which originated in Russia. There the Revolution was inevitable and, though I did not agree with the excesses which took place then, I tried to understand the reasons why. It is only when the sufferings of others come nearer to one's own door or even affect one quite closely, one begins to have serious doubts. And the behaviour of the Russian soldiers after they had entered Berlin as victors started my doubts. When she was raped by a Russian soldier, my eldest half-sister, a deeply convinced Communist, considered that this was part of her penance for the cruelty of the Nazis in Russia. How far can logic take us?

I had wanted to go to Russia ever since my first contact through employment in the Russian Embassy. No other country in the world held out such enchantment. But since the end of the last war this image received some very hard knocks. The treason trials, though I did not understand them, caused the first doubts in my mind. But the whole terrible affair of the Stalin terror was, it appeared, something that only Russians could understand. Then came the Hungarian disaster of 1956 and the evil influence the Russian Communists had in Hungary. A man's word is his bond, whether it is given by one man or by several of the same persuasion, and the brutal murder of Nagy and other members of his Government made me feel furiously angry, and completely wiped out my desire to go to Russia. At long last my husband persuaded me to go with him and so it has come about that I am asked to join him in giving my impressions as an addition to his book.

People better able to express themselves than I have gone to Russia and have written books about it. There have been those who have gone determined to find fault with everything they might see. I have often been angry when I read their books, because they often compared Russia with countries which had neither had a revolution, nor had been devastated by war, nor had suffered from the terrible scourge of 'scorched earth'. Poverty is a ruthless task-master, and the economy of a large country like Russia demands unending sacrifice. On the other hand, some very good friends have told me that existing conditions in Russia are much better than they were before 1914, and I can only believe them.

The war ended fifteen years ago, however, and I feel that the lot of the Russian people could have been improved beyond what it is now. But I found that young Communists in Russia did not look on it this way. I had to be very careful about what I said to our young Intourist guides in Leningrad, Moscow and Kieff, because they felt intensely patriotic and found no fault with their Government. What did surprise me was the unexpected attitude of the young man, who was our guide in Leningrad, towards Peter the Great. My innocent question as to whether Peter the Great (of whom I had never seen a picture) had been a small man met with real indignation, and he took trouble to show me the real size of the man by taking me to a gallery where some of his clothes were kept and a large stick was shown which was notched at the real height of the Tsar. Though a Communist, he evidently felt very proud of Peter the Great. Another piece of evidence which showed appreciation of Peter the Great was a vase of fresh flowers on his tomb in the Church of St Peter and St Paul. Yet the same young man showed his disgust at my request to find, if possible, a print of a picture which I had seen in the private office of a 'White Russian' here in London, and which I would have liked to buy if possible. When, at the end of a long tour through the Russian Museum, I found myself standing before the very original of this picture, his distaste knew no bounds. The very name of the picture, 'Wife of a Merchant behind the Samovar', had so little to do with modern Russia, he could only condemn it. And when my husband dared to express the thoughts that he felt when looking at another picture of a man he might have met, Communist logic went quite haywire. To begin with, the man was so obviously a bourgeois and therefore one ought not to admit one had known him, and who was my husband anyhow? He was a 'cunneusser' (connoisseur) and it was obvious to him my husband was not.

The old part of Leningrad which was formerly St Petersburg is without doubt very beautiful. I fear, however, that the average Russian citizen has not much interest in beauty or elegance. The Winter Palace and the Hermitage are full of lovely things and it is an obvious desire of the Government to make the Russian people conscious of the beauty of their heritage by encouraging almost continuous sight-seeing tours. It must be hoped that the men and women who go and look at these countless treasures will in time realize that we cannot live and appreciate the present without appreciating the past. One does not have to deny the past while being a live member of the present, but not so among the youth of the USSR. They are full of contradictions and cannot bear to have this pointed out to them. They feel they *have* to be right and are intolerant of opinions which differ from those which they have been taught to accept as the only right ones. The young man who acted as our guide in Leningrad and the young girl in Moscow, and later on the young woman in Kieff, all had their patter right. There must be no deviation, indeed no personal opinion. To think along independent lines would be heresy and, come to think of it, that is exactly how I behaved when I was young. I am now nearly three times as old and have learned that *not* all that comes from Russia is of necessity good, that the leaders of the Russian Communist Party are apt to break their word, that they have great contempt for human suffering, that they are capable of betraying their most devoted followers, and that in consequence of all this it is as hard to continue to believe in the Socialist ideal as it was for the early Christians to continue to believe in their God when they were thrown into the lion's cage. Most of us can put up with poverty, but I find it very hard to forgive betrayal as shown in Stalin's reign of terror. I must therefore admit being prejudiced in anything I saw about Russia and conditions as they strike us now.

The first callous remarks, so it strikes me, which many people make when they enter Russia are about the size of the women. It cannot be denied that a great number of Russian women are larger than those of other nations and it is not unreasonable to ask why this is so. I well remember how the women of this country found it hard to keep their weight down and how difficult it was to stick to a slimming diet during the last war. Bread and potatoes are the staple food in Russia, as it was in this country during the war and for a long time after the end of it. Russian women have to work very hard. They eat great quantities of bread, which by the way is excellent. They have little contact with the Western world and have not that urge to slim, neither have they the desire to be able to wear the latest French fashions. They have neither the time nor the money, nor the knowledge, and they do not want to imitate their Western sisters. The need to work is greater than any of these, and the appetite which is caused by hard work is easiest stilled by eating large quantities of bread and their much-favoured 'borsch'. To laugh at them, therefore, is to lack an understanding of their needs. When one is poor, the most important thing is to fill one's stomach. Beauty is a very secondary consideration.

It is impossible to say anything in praise of that part of Leningrad which is mainly occupied by the working people. While money is being spent on keeping the old palaces in good order, the dwelling-houses are much neglected. Had I thought a little longer before asking our guide, I might have drawn my own conclusions. Since there has been no private ownership in houses till recently, it is the local councils who say what amount of repairs is permitted to these State-owned houses, and it struck me that permission was being given to very little. The surfaces of most old dwelling-houses were peeling, doors and windows needed painting, many windows were broken and many had been sealed with paper. When I asked whether occupiers of the flats were permitted to pay for glass to repair broken windows, the answer was yes, but I was indignantly asked at the same time as to whether I had seen any broken windows? Our young guide had quite a few mental black spots, and the many holes in the walls and windows no longer made any impression on his mind.

In the very centre of Leningrad stands the fortress of St Peter and St Paul and in its grounds stands the first of all political prisons. It is a gruesome reminder of the Tsarist régime and people are constantly taken round and shown the cells, the kind of garb the men and women were compelled to wear, the manacles which they had to carry on their way to Siberia and the terrible punishment cells. These are equal to the dungeons of the Middle Ages, because a prisoner might be deprived of all light by covering the window with a heavy wooden shutter within which a very small six-inch square could be opened if the prisoner was not considered too dangerous. We were shown the effect it had when completely closed, and to people who suffered from claustrophobia it must have been worse than a nightmare. In front of one of the buildings we were shown the 'dancing ground', where a particularly obstreperous prisoner would be tied to a post standing on ground covered with broken glass. While the prisoner was beaten and tried to escape his tormenter, he would try also to avoid the broken glass at his feet; hence he looked as if he was dancing. Could brutality go further? Yet within a few steps one could admire the lovely and lofty church which is so elegant that our young guide compared it to a ballroom. But cruelty had its corner even there. The son of Peter the Great, so we were told, was buried under the stairs leading to the belfry (pronounced by the same young guide as bel-fry) in order that he should be humiliated by the fact that the men working on the tower should walk over his grave. But, as I have said before, a bunch of fresh flowers was placed on Peter the Great's tomb.

The cathedral of St Isaac is very well looked after. But we were told that this care was not only taken to protect the substance, but to honour the memory of the men who lost their lives while building it. The dome is covered with gold leaf; to secure gold leaf to copper plates, the copper had to be heated to melt the mercury to which the leaf was attached; the resulting fumes killed many men. It is this use of precious and semi-precious metal and stone which makes this cathedral look as if it had been painted yesterday. My first impression was one of garishness, until I took a better look. The columns in front of the iconostas are carved out of lapis lazuli and malachite and the mosaics are covered with gold leaf. Being the genuine material, they have kept their natural colour and to the uninformed eye look like paint put on too loudly. One of the larger-than-life mosaics had been taken down for cleaning and left standing at ground-level for all to see.

The hotel in which we stayed had been built in 1912. The plumbing was as old and lived up to it. But whereas the public which used this hotel in 1912 were those who were used to keeping 'the lower orders' in their place, 'the lower orders' now filled it in large numbers, mainly for conferences. This hotel was theirs, and there was no feeling of uncertainty in their behaviour. Having been hopeful for no more than a bedroom and perhaps a bathroom, we were given a suite of five rooms. Designed and arranged in such a manner, one could play hide and seek in them.

Much has been said in the past about the suppression of religion in Russia. To make sure and in opposition to our young guide, we went to one of the churches. Great was our surprise when we found the church not only full, but crammed on two floors! I have never seen a church in which two services went on simultaneously. The people were standing elbow to elbow, praying and chanting, the priests in all their glory leading the congregation in prayer, and an enthusiastic congregation taking it all in. In front of me an elderly and pathetically thin woman prostrated herself for many minutes at a time, regardless of the movement around her. It would be untrue to say there were many soldiers among them, but there were some. There was a constant coming and going and women pushed their children forward to reach the priest, who would bless them when the service was over. When I later told our guide in Kieff that I had seen soldiers in a church in Leningrad, she tried to laugh it off by saying that they had been sight-seeing!

On our arrival in Moscow we were taken to the newest skyscraper hotel. We would have preferred to be nearer the centre of the city, but one has little choice with Intourist. Although we were told that there were stairs from floor to floor, we never discovered them and I shudder to think of a fire in such a building where lifts were, as a rule, overloaded. Here again we had hoped for a bedroom with perhaps a bathroom, but Intourist thought differently and gave us three large rooms and *two* bathrooms. The rooms were exquisitely clean, and the very large comrade who took us to our quarters most friendly and obliging.

Our first endeavour was to see Lenin's tomb and the Lenin Museum. One cannot escape Lenin. Not that I would have wanted to, but Peter the Great certainly takes second place. Wherever you look there is a picture of Lenin or a bust of Lenin. He is everywhere. Having become acquainted with his work and with the utter simplicity in which he lived, that is not surprising. The Tsars and the nobility left their mark in rich and beautiful buildings. Lenin's simple rooms are a striking example of how a great leader ought to live. In Leningrad, in the Smolny Institute, we were shown the humble bedroom curtained off from the rest of the room where he interviewed peasants and representatives of the people who wanted his help. In Moscow one cannot help being in the presence of Lenin; one sees him everywhere. One looks at his enshrined body, one sees his pictures, one can see his death mask in the Lenin Museum, one can read his speeches, one can see a film, and finally, one can hear his voice. It is a curiously light baritone voice and it moved me to tears to hear it.

What impressed me in Moscow was the great number of people rushing about in groups, and what astonished me too was the condition of their footwear. I began to be fascinated by the number of hurrying feet and the type of boots and shoes they wore. With very few exceptions they were ill-cared for and most of them were very clumsy. Men wore pale grey shoes of a sort which no Englishman would be seen dead in. All the clothes worn by women were dark and dowdy. Most women wore head-shawls; hats were the exception. And they were of the kind which were out of fashion long ago. Hats in shop-windows were like those sold here at jumble sales, but that did not affect the price. I am saying all this, not in a spirit of criticism, but because I am sorry it is so. The splendour of the past in the time of the Tsars compares strikingly with the drabness of the present. In the past no money was spared to build beautiful churches and palaces, but very little was spent on houses and schools for the poor. The simple beauty of the Smolny Institute was created for the benefit of rich men's daughters. Now money is spent on education, on schools and universities. Yet again the old people could be better provided for. We saw many old men and women begging inside and outside all churches. When I asked for an explanation, I was told they could, if they wanted, ask to be sent to an old people's home where they would be provided for. The young people to whom we talked about this were indifferent towards them. We heard the old story that many of them probably had thousands of roubles under their pillows when found dead in their bed. I got quite angry with one of our young girl interpreters who could not see that a hungry old woman is a hungry old woman, and needed help, whether she had roubles under the pillow or not, and I told her that in this country the so-called means test was one of the first things abolished by the Labour Party.

Owing to a misunderstanding between Intourist and the Police, we were stopped on our trip to Vladimir, where we had wanted to go and see some old churches. Our disappointment and anger was so great that we thought of cancelling our journey to Kieff. An official who had been helpful to my husband was sufficiently impressed by our anger and tried to make up for our disappointment by suggesting that we might like to be shown most of that part of the Kremlin which is reserved for VIPs. In retrospect one might bless the policeman who stopped us from going to Vladimir, because had he not done so we would never have seen all the splendour of the Kremlin; the splendour of the past and the simplicity of the present, the splendour of the Tsars since Ivan the Terrible up till the last Tsar, and the simplicity of Lenin's flat where he lived with his wife and some nephews. The contrast was very great. It seemed like divine justice when only the outward apparel of past Tsars was shown in many of the great halls, whereas not enough could be shown of everything pertaining to Lenin. His was the place of honour everywhere. Particularly touching was the small kitchen in which he would prepare a meal for himself if he came home late and would not allow a member of the staff to sit up late to do it for him. His slightly chipped tea-cup impressed me as much as did the ivory and diamond embossed sceptre of Ivan the Terrible which is shown in the armoury.

A visit to GUM, the multiple stores which we are sometimes shown on TV, did not reveal anything outstanding. All articles are expensive and none exceeded ours in this country in quality or design. An amusing fact revealed itself when I went back to the stores to buy a small article. I found the stores closed and on enquiry was told that it was 'sanitation day', when everything was cleaned and the public excluded.

Perhaps it is wrong to single out a performance of 'Anna Karenina' as outstanding for our intellectual entertainment. Everything done in Russia is done for one's intellectual entertainment, but this stood out for both of us as something which we really enjoyed; not the sadness of the story, but the manner of the production and the naturalness with which Russian actors act. I can say it in no other way.

Our third and last stop was at Kieff. Though very many memories came to my husband's mind in other parts of Russia which we visited, this visit to Kieff did, I believe, give him the most pleasure. He had visited a collective farm fourteen years earlier and he had now a chance to make a comparison. Did the peasants like being members of a collective farm and had they been successful? He found that they were glad to be members and that the system had on the whole been successful. By good luck we were taken to the same farm and the manager most obligingly answered all questions which were put to him. We were taken a complete round of visits to all farm buildings, were shown all the pig-sties, hen-houses, all the machinery, the harvesters, tractors, etc., and the many young girls who seemed to spend their time washing the frame-work which divided the pig-sties in a very leisurely fashion. We were shown the small room in which the young women could rest if they wanted to, but it seemed to me that the room was never used at all. It was tidy and smelt cold; old magazines lay on the table and they were the same ones I had seen on the Russian boat coming across, and there was no sign of any activity at all. I dared to ask the manager whether anything was done to entertain the girls and the wives who were working on the farm, and I got the very cold answer (through the interpreter) that since women were the equals of men, they shared their work, and that would seem to be enough! I asked no more.

We visited the village school and saw a great many children at play. This school was not big enough to teach all children during the morning and there had to be a shift system. All the children—and it was the same everywhere else—looked well and happy. None of them had that fear of the teacher which I associated with my youth in Germany. I noticed the same free and easy behaviour in a bigger and modern school in Kieff and it made me glad. One fact stood out, however, which continually impressed itself on my mind: the colourless life and drab clothes of men, women and children. I expected to see frocks and embroidered blouses, but the only place one could see them was on the stage. In Kieff I found the only shop where one could buy these things, but it did not appear to be well known.

Our visit to the collective farm ended on a very pleasant note. Fourteen years ago my husband had been entertained by one of the peasants and his wife. The same two people were still living there, and when they heard he had returned they sent a message, inviting us to a meal. It was spontaneous and generously done. Not only ourselves, but the two guides and the farm manager as well. Many questions were asked, and the talk seemed endless. If anyone wonders why we had two guides, the answer is that we had been disappointed at being denied our visit to Vladimir, so our little guide, whom we liked so much, had been detailed by Intourist to accompany us for the rest of our journey, and she even had to take us as far as Brest-Litovsk, where we said good-bye to her and to Russia.

But that did not mean that we had seen the last of the influence Russia exercises over her neighbours and especially over conditions in Germany, which is where we went next. Our arrival in Berlin of necessity took place in the eastern part of the city. The taxi-driver had no hesitation in taking us through the Brandenburger Tor. We had only to hold up our wonderful British passports and we were waved on. Do the owners of British passports know the magic of their being able to show it at critical moments? I am reminded of a night of terror after Hitler had marched into Vienna and my daughter and I had to leave Austria, and on crossing the frontier at midnight, when many personal tragedies happened to people not in possession of British passports, we were waved on at sight of this magical little blue book. Twenty years later the almighty Russian-inspired German policeman waved us through the Brandenburger Tor. Since the new Russian Embassy is situated at Unter den Linden, it stands to reason that the Russian Government would not allow this splendid building to be built among rubble. The rubble takes its place where it belongs, in the miserable little back-streets, miles of them, untouched and, it seems, forgotten. As soon as we emerged from the long chausée, which divides the West from East, one *wanted* to take notice. Although it has been impossible to rebuild a city as shattered as Berlin, there was a pulsating feeling of Life. Roads had been widened, new large buildings were going up everywhere, the people were *alive*. Our hotel had given itself a proud British name and, though by no means boasting of the newest and biggest so-called comforts, it proved to be a well-run, pleasant and extremely clean place to stay in. What struck me, being a housewife, was the startling difference in the condition of the bathroom. Across the WC lay folded a strip of paper informing us in four languages that this WC had been cleaned according to the most up-to-date standard of cleanliness, and it looked it. Being mindful of the WCs we had encountered in Russia, one could not but notice the difference.

Berlin has been described by most strangers as an unattractive city. One cannot quarrel over that. To me it is the most alive city, full of memories and, to my own mind, incomparable. It represents my first step in becoming a seeing and learning adult. I learned to think; I began to see and my first impression of what Socialism means began there. I was unhappy in Berlin, I was happy in Berlin. I married there and my children were born there. I love Berlin. The architecture of the late nineteenth century meant little to me. I did not understand anything of architecture when young. I left Berlin when still young and now that I met the city again after such a disastrous interval, I only wanted to see what had happened to alter Berlin. The same somewhat crude sense of humour still existed. I was glad to be greeted by the railway porter and the taxi-driver with the same dry expressions of what they thought could be done to get us across the 'border'. It is a ludicrous thought that someone on one side of the Brandenburger Tor, wanting to send a parcel to a friend on the other side of the Tor, must write out a customs declaration. Or that an over-officious ticket collector at a railway station in the Eastern section should be allowed to put his nose into the shopping-bag of a housewife and confiscate the forbidden oranges she has managed to buy in the West.

Our first endeavour was to see what was needed to get a permit to visit my home-town situated in the East Zone. We were taken by a well-versed taxi-owner to the police station where such permits were handed out. In the corridor of the building posters told us that permits to 'leave for the Ausland' would be given here, and our driver snorted and said 'Halberstadt, Ausland!' and no more. An officious young policeman received us and asked us why we wanted to go to Halberstadt. He could not quite believe that we wanted to go mainly because I wanted to visit the town for the love of it, but gave us eight forms to fill up each requiring a photograph, and then asked us the astonishing question: were we prepared to pay for it? Since that was self-evident and he noticed my surprise, he asked: would we be prepared to pay for a *Betreuer*, i.e. spy, and at that I declared with much vehemence that I would *not*. He dismissed us without giving us the promise of a permit, but asked us to call again a day later. I for one was not at all surprised that we were given the permit, but now we had to go to two more offices to get our 'visas', and our tickets. And it was this journey which brought home to me more than anything else since we had left Russia that we were in fact still travelling by permission of a kind of German-Russian Intourist.

We were permitted to stay only two days, but the condition in which I found my old home town was such that I could not have taken advantage of this generous permission. The influence of the Kremlin, or could one say the lack of good influence over such unhappy little towns as Halberstadt, was visible immediately. My memories of this mediaeval town were not prepared for the shock which lay in store for us. The centre was completely destroyed, all its lovely old buildings gone, and not a stone had been raised to restore any semblance of what once had been. No funds have been provided to repair the war damage and the people stood at certain points in the wilderness of what once had been their glory, waiting for a tram-car or ramshackle bus. A little church in an out-of-the-way village could not be painted inside because the hole in the roof could not be repaired for lack of bricks, and they were not granted because it was only a little church without national significance. The money for the paint was available, but the bricks were not forthcoming. Whatever part of the town had not been destroyed looked so sadly down-at-heel, I had to choke back my tears. No paint has been used, no building material of any kind has been allowed to make good the damage. The people are silent and look dejected, and the only building which has been repaired is the Dom. People and their needs are of no importance, their pride is not considered. The Government of the Eastern Zone, which acts entirely on the instructions of its overlords from Russia, has no pride either, and the shameful result can be observed everywhere. Fourteen years since the end of war is a long time and much good could have been done in that interval.

Germany has always been a clean country; cleanliness like obedience was second nature to the Germans. Our train journey from Berlin to Halberstadt was in every respect like any journey in Russia; a loudspeaker in every compartment, but dirt everywhere and the wcs unusable. How could one shut ones eyes to the evidence of mismanagement in one part of Germany and not appreciate the completely different conditions in the other?

One may, if one liked, ignore the dirt, but one cannot ignore the almost complete absence of rebuilding for the people and the rebuilding of famous old civic centres. West Berlin, which, so it has always been said, is built on sand, is endeavouring the impossible, and many so-called High-houses are rising, carefully not called skyscrapers, on what seems to be a sea of sand. That dangerous-looking ruin of the Gedächtniskirche (Kaiser William Memorial Church) is being tunnelled around for a new underground railway. A group of architects of international fame have redesigned a completely destroyed quarter near the Tiergarten and have shown more imagination than many architects have done elsewhere. There is a sameness of design in the Stalin Allée as there is in the new blocks of buildings in Moscow and in the new Russian Embassy at Unter den Linden. That building looks grand, and that is the best one can say about it. The comparison which struck us, in the train journey from the West to the Eastern Zone, was that there were endless streamers across roads and on many public buildings announcing, as in the days of Hitler, that the good, which was being created, was due to the 'Democratic' Government of Ulbricht and Grotewohl, to which I add, by permission of Russia. And then one looked and wondered where was the evidence of it all?

I do not know what has moved some former well-known Communists to leave the Communist Party and tell the world of their experiences. My own feelings I would like to compare to those of the first Christians, who preferred to go into the lion's cage and be devoured rather than deny their belief in God. It is not a *belief* I have that Socialism has been and is essential, it is a firm *conviction*. I hope I shall not be accused of blasphemy when I say that I think Jesus was the first Socialist, and as His first followers did not deny Him, so I do not deny Socialism. But I despise lack of pride in the German heads of Government of the Eastern Zone, and I despise treachery, which has become an article of use to the Russian Government.

APPENDIX

Quotations by prominent men of the West about Russia in the past and by Russians about themselves and their rôle in Europe

1. In 1547, i.e. ninety-four years after the capture of Constantinople by the Ottoman Turks, Abbot Theophilus of the Monastery at Pskov wrote to Tsar Basil III in Moscow: 'The church of Old Rome fell because of heresy and the gates of the second Rome at Constantinople have been hewn down by the infidel Turks. But the church of the new Rome shines brighter than the sun in the universe. Two Romes have fallen but a third (in Moscow) stands fast. A fourth there cannot be.'

2. Despatch of British Admiral in the Baltic in 1719 after Peter the Great had defeated the Swedes at Poltawa and was building up a naval force based on Kronstadt: 'A dangerous power is arising in the East which the nations of Western Europe must watch and guard against.'
Reply of the Secretary of State for the Admiralty to Admiral in the Baltic: 'The Russian fleet will disturb the world while it is stirred by ambition and revenge.' He added that in certain circumstances the Admiral was to engage and sink the Russian fleet.

3. After the defeat of Napoleon and the peace signed at the Congress of Vienna, Austrian fear of Russia became very great. Britain then acted as mediator, and Lord Castlereagh wrote to Prince Metternich in 1816 the following: 'Prince Metternich mistakes the sentiments of this Court if he supposes that we urge him to adopt either a submissive or a conceding policy to Russia. It is not in the maintenance of her just pretensions that we would discourage Austria. We only wish to moderate that "Cri de Bureau" against Russia which must, to a degree, exist in all governments against a state so powerful as Russia has lately become, but which prevails (perhaps not unnaturally) amongst Austrian agents at home and abroad. We conscientiously believe that if this is not repressed, and that with some vigour, by those at the head of affairs, there is a direct and rapid tendency to create the very danger which it would attempt to avoid.'
Passage in Webster's *Foreign Policy of Lord Castlereagh (1815-1822)*, page 97: 'What puzzled contemporaries was how to reconcile Russian actions in Italy, Spain and Germany with these professions of a desire for the closest co-operation with other Great Powers.

These professions were, it is true, mixed up with assertions and claims which betray all the symptoms of a disordered intellect or, at least, that kind of inspiration which is closely akin to madness.'

Passage in *Cambridge History of British Foreign Policy* on situation in Europe after the end of the Napoleonic Wars in 1815: 'It was indeed precisely this enigmatic attitude of the Tsar, not towards the question of Turkey only, which kept the chanceries in a flutter of excitement and apprehension. His talk (the Tsar) was of peace; but he maintained his huge armies in being and concentrated for the most part on the Western and Balkan fronts of his Empire. He preached unctuously the gospel of fraternity and mutual trust, but his agents were meanwhile carrying on dark intrigues in every court and country of Europe.'

4. In 1839 the Marquis de Custine, a French aristocrat whose father had perished in the French Revolution, went to Russia in the hopes of finding a strong government where aristocratic society was preserved. In spite of his hatred of Revolution, he soon found that his 'Frenchness' and Western culture were stronger than any affection he could find for Russia. In his book *La Russie en Trente Neuf*, published in 1843, he writes: 'If the Russians have better diplomats than peoples with a more advanced civilization, it is because our newspapers warn them of everything which is happening and which is being planned in our country and instead of prudently hiding our weaknesses, we zealously reveal them every morning. On the other hand, their Byzantine policy of working in the shadow carefully conceals from us what is being thought, what is being done and what is feared in their countries. We walk in full daylight, they advance under cover; the game is not played on equal terms. The ignorance in which they leave us blinds us; our sincerity enlightens them. We have the weakness of gossiping, they have the strength of secrecy. Herein above all lies their skill.'

On page 50 of the same book he wrote: 'A new Roman Empire has arisen on the ashes of the old Greek Empire, an Empire in which force is accompanied by artfulness and ferocity. . . . The Russians see Europe as a prey which will be delivered to them sooner or later by its internal chaos. They foment among us anarchy in the hope of profiting by the corruption caused by them. Such is the history of Poland. And Europe is going the way of Poland. It is enervated by a vain liberalism, because those remain strong who are not free.'

Also in 1839, M. Emile Montegut wrote in the *Revue des Deux Mondes*: 'All people who aspire to universal domination announce their intentions openly. . . . The first people who do not avow their aims are the Russians. This enables them to become easily and without danger to themselves aggressive. . . . To resist Russia effectively armies are not the only necessity. It is necessary to resist her with the spirit and with ideas.'

5. In 1852 the United States Ambassador to Russia, Neill S. Brown, reports to Washington: 'A strong superstition prevails among the Russians that they are predestined to conquer the world and the prayers of the priests and the church are mingled with requests to hasten and consummate this Divine Mission.'

In another despatch he writes: 'The Russian mind seems to be naturally distrustful and this is especially so of Russian officials. Access by all foreigners is now difficult and will require but little more to render it impracticable. Secrecy and mystery characterize everything.'

6. In 1853 Karl Marx, in exile, wrote regularly in the *New York Tribune* and one of his articles contains the following passages: 'Russia is decidedly a conquering nation and was so for a century, until the great movement of 1789 called into potent activity an antagonist of formidable nature. I mean the European revolution, the explosive force of democratic ideas and mass native thirst for freedom. But let Russia get possession of Turkey and her strength is increased nearly half. The arrest of the Russian scheme of annexation is a matter of the highest moment.'

In another article he writes: 'Russia may seem obstinately and deeply attached to certain fixed ideas, but as soon as the other Powers resist in a determined and united way, they will find that Russia will accept a modest retreat.'

7. On June 8, 1880, in Moscow, Dostoiefsky delivered a public speech at the unveiling of the memorial to the great writer and dramatist, Pushkin. The following are extracts of the speech which give some idea how Dostoiefsky was reacting at that time towards Western Europe: 'To be a typical Russian means to become a brother of all people. All that Slavophilism on the one hand and the Western School of thought on the other that is with us is a great instinct which is both historical and necessary. For the typical Russian, Europe and the fate of its great Aryan people is as dear to us as Russia herself, as the fate, in fact, of our Russian soil, because our fate is bound up with the rest of the world. . . . Look at our history after Peter's reforms and you will find already the signs and traces of that thought, of that dream of a commune with the European people, even in our national politics. What else did Russia do in the last two-hundred years but serve Europe, perhaps more than the Europeans them-

selves. . . . The people of Europe do not know how dear they are to us. To be a typical Russian actually means striving to conciliate European controversies and to show the way out of European distress in our own Russian spirit.'

8. In 1903, the Foreign Minister of Nicholas II, Count Muravieff, made a speech containing the following passage: 'I believe that Russia has a special mission such as no other people in the world, not only in Asia but also in Europe. We Russians bear upon our shoulders the New Age; we come to relieve the tired men.'

9. In 1947 the Russian philosopher, Nicholas Berdyaev, a friend of Lenin, not a Communist, in *The Russian Idea* (Bles, Centenary Press, London, 1947), wrote on page 124: 'There is a sort of law of dialectic development in accordance with which what is base and evil is, within a certain time, not destroyed but overcome (Aufheben) and all the positive good of the preceding period enters into the overcoming of it. Dostoievsky brings us to this thought; he reveals the metaphysical depths of the Russian theme of social right. In his view it is linked with Russian Messianism. The Russian people as a people are God-bearers. They ought to solve the social problem better than the West, but great temptations lie in wait for this people.'

On page 193: 'Apocalypse has always played a great part both among the masses of our people and the highest cultural level, among Russian writers and thinkers. In our thought the eschatological problem takes an immeasurably greater place than in the thinking of the West and this is connected with the very structure of Russian consciousness, which is but little adapted and little inclined to cling to vanished forms of the intervening culture.'

On page 217: 'Both Moscow the Third Rome and Moscow the Third International are connected with the Russian messianic idea. They represent a distorted form of it. Never in history, I think, has there been a people which has combined such opposites in its history.'

On page 218: 'The Russian idea was recognized in various forms in the nineteenth century, but found itself in profound conflict with Russian history as it was built up by forces which held sway in it. In this lies the tragic element in the historical destiny of Russia and also the complexity of our subject.'

On page 255: 'It must be remembered that the nature of the Russians is highly polarized. On the one side it is humble and self-denying; on the other side there is revolt aroused by pity and demanding justice; on the one hand sympathy, compassion, on the other hand the possibility of cruelty. . . . Mysticism of race and blood is alien to the Russians, but the mysticism of the soil is very much akin to them. The Russian people, in accordance with its internal Idea, has no love for the ordering of this earthly city and struggles towards a city that is to come, towards the new Jerusalem. But the new Jerusalem is not to be torn away from the vast Russian land. The new Jerusalem is linked with it and it, the soil, leads to the new Jerusalem. The spirit of community and the brotherhood of Mankind are a necessity for the new Jerusalem and for the attainment of this it is still endeavouring to have the experience of an era of the Holy Spirit in which there will be a new Revelation about society. For this the way is being prepared in Russia.'

INDEX

Academy of Science in Kieff, 71
Agrarian revolution in Ukraine, 79
..system in old Ukraine, 78, 79
Agricultural production and output per man, 81—4
Anna Karenina, 62, 118
Art and drama in Russia, 34, 35, 62, 63

Baltika, 15, 20
Bauman Institute, 49, 50
Berdyaev, Nicholas, 126
Berlin humour, 90, 120
    modern architecture, 90, 122
    rebuilding of West, 89, 90, 119
    relations with Communist East, 91, 92
    scenes of former struggles, 95-8
    shops and prices, 100
    visits to old friends, 93-5
Bernstein, Edward, 96
Bison, European, 71
'Bolshoi' Opera House, 46, 47
Bombing of Halberstadt, 106, 107
Breitscheid, Rudolph, 96, 110
Brest-Litovsk, negotiations at, 33, 45
Bureaucracy in Russia, 44
Byzantine Christianity in Russia, 73, 74

Carpathians, 87
Castlereagh, Lord, 123
Cathedral at Halberstadt, 107
Central Asia, Russian, 57
Chekhoff, 62
Collective farm, individual allotments, 85
    production and output per man, 81-4
    system, 79-86
    visit to, 81-6, 118
Collective farming in Central Germany, 104, 105
Communism, activities in Asia and Africa, 40, 41
    and collective farming, 79-86
    and World Revolution, 37, 38, 40 75, 76
    in East Germany, 108, 109, 121
    role in Central Asia, 58
    role in Russia, 56
Communist attitude to art and architecture, 72
    influence in Germany, 94, 98, 99, 100
    youth in Russia, 113
Communist Party membership, 40
Communists and revolt of Left S.R.s and Anarchists, 47
Custine, Marquis de, 124

Dibelius, Bishop, 101
Dnieper, river, 68, 87
Dostoiefsky, 76, 125
Duditseff, novel of, 39, 56
Duma, Imperial, 33

Index

East German Republic, 91, 92, 102
Education, Russian, 48, 50, 51, 118, 119
  technical, 48, 49
  technological, 49, 50
  visit to primary school, 70, 118
Eisner, Kurt, 98
Exhibition, Industrial and Agricultural, in Moscow, 57
Exhibition of Ukrainian agriculture, 69

Factory, visit to, 53-5
Finland, relations with Russia, 16-19
Finnish tribes in Russia, 87
Fortress of Peter and Paul, 28, 29, 112, 114
Frederick the Great, 103
Frunze, 70, 71

German Communism and resistance to Russian influence, 94, 97, 98, 99, 100
German Communism today, 108, 109
Germany, division of, 92, 108, 109
Germany, revolutionary struggles, 97, 98
Germany's future, 109
Glinka, 16
Goethe, 76
Gogol, 75, 76, 80
Granovietaya Palata, 61

Haase, Hugo, 98
Halberstadt, 102-8
Helsinki, 16-19

Hermitage, 35
Housing conditions in Russia, 38, 39, 52, 53

Industrial organisation, 53-5
Institute for World Economy and International Relations, 38, 40
Inter-Parliamentary Union, 37, 60, 61
Intourist, 15, 20, 60, 61
  ..guides, 36
Ivan the terrible, 59, 61, 81, 117

Kazakistan, 57
Kazan cathedral, 27
Khmelnitzky, Bogdan, 65, 73
Kieff, 64-76
  ..parks of, 69, 75
Kirghisia, 57
Kollontai, Madame, 34
Kremlin, 48, 61, 117
Krushchev, Mr, 39, 43, 50, 85
Kutuzov Museum, 48

Landlords in Ukraine, 78, 79
Ledebour, Georg, 96
Lenin, comparison with Peter the Great, 29
  famous speech of, 45
  his role in Peace Treaty crisis, 33, 34
  his role in Revolution, 31, 32
  homage paid to, 53, 116, 117
  Museum, 116
  my interview with, 61
  rooms at Kremlin, 61, 117
  rooms at Smolny, 31, 116
  theory of government, 32, 94

Leningrad, architecture, 27
  art and drama, 34, 35
  atmosphere of, 20, 21
  housing, 23, 24
  industrial activities, 24
  Kazan cathedral, 22
  my experiences during Revolution in, 24, 25
  my former flat in, 24, 25
  Orthodox churches in, 28
  prices, 22
  shops and businesses, 21
  timber trade, 26, 27
Liebknecht, Karl, 97, 110
Literature, average popular, 39
Livestock in Russia, 70, 71, 83
Lutheran church in Berlin, 100, 101
Lvov (Lemberg), 77

Magdeburg, 103
Manchester Guardian, 31, 77
Marienkirche, Berlin, 100, 101
Marinsky Theatre, 34
Marx, Karl, 125
Metternich, Prince, 123
Military Revolutionary Committee, 32
Milk production in Ukraine, 83, 84
Mogil, Peter, 73
Mongol invasion of Russia, 64, 65, 73, 75
Montegut, Emile, 124
Moscow Art Theatre, 62
  factory conditions, 53-5
  housing, 38, 52, 53
  life in, 37-9
  past reminiscences of, 37, 38, 45, 47
  University, 48

Moslem population of Russian Asia, 57, 58
Muravieff, Count, 126

Nevsky Prospect, 21
Novo-Divichi Monastery, 47

Ornithology in Ukraine, 71
Orthodox churches, 28
Ostankino, Technical Institute, 48

Pasternak, 55
Peasant standard of living on collective farms, 82, 84
Pechenegs, 73
Pechersky Lavra in Kieff, 72
Peter the Great, 28, 29, 32, 65, 73, 74, 112, 123
Polish collective farms, 105
Polish former landlords in Ukraine, 65, 78, 79
Poltawa, battle of, 65, 74, 123
Potsdam, 103
Pripet marshes, 87
'Prostor', 75
Pushkin, 16, 34, 62, 80, 125

Queen of Spades opera, 34, 35

Rathenau, Walter, 98
Religious services, 28, 74, 75, 115, 116
Roza Luxembourg, opposition to Lenin, 32, 94, 97
Russia, change in world outlook, 37, 38
  historical background of, 29, 30, 56

industrial organisation, 53, 54, 55
planned economy and free economy of West, 44
present standard of living, 39
stages of economic growth, 41, 42, 43
Russian art and drama, 34, 35, 62, 63
  Baltic Fleet, 17
  bureaucracy, 44
  character, 16
  education, strength and weakness, 48-51
  Gallery, 35
  influence on German Communism, 94
  outlook on life, 75, 76
  science, 48, 71
  women's dress and style, 23, 114, 116, 117, 119
  women, food and figure, 113, 114

Science, Academy of, 71
Smolny Institute, scenes in Revolution, 30, 31
'Sobornost', 16
Solodovnikoff, M., 40
Sovnarhoz, 54
St Isaacs, 20, 27, 115
St Sophia in Kieff, 72-4
St Vladimir in Kieff, 72, 74
Stalin at Smolny, 31
  and régime of terror, 55, 72, 112
  and Socialist Soviet Motherland, 46
  conflict with Trotsky, 45
Stolypin, land reforms of, 79, 80
Sukhumlinoff, General, 28, 29
Sverdloff, 31

Tadjikistan, 57
Taurida Palace, 32, 34
Technical education, 48, 49
Technological education, 49, 50
Theophilus, Abbot of Pskov, 123
Timber Export Trust, 58
Timber trade in Russia, my connections, 26
Timber trade in Russia, contacts in Moscow, 58, 59
Tolstoy, Alexei, 81
Tolstoy, Sergei, my acquaintance with, 47
'Toska', 75, 76
Trade Unions, 54, 55
Tretiakoff Gallery, 35, 62, 63
Trotsky, 31, 45
  conflict with Stalin, 45
Tsarist régime, popular attitude to, 37
Tschaikowsky, 16, 34
Turkestan, 57

Ukranian architecture, 67, 72, 73, 74
  art and drama, 67, 74
  culture, 66, 67, 73
  early civilization, 64, 65, 73
  government, 66
  language, 65, 66
  Ministry of Agriculture, 69
  women's dress and style, 68
Uniate church, 78
University, meeting with professors, 55, 56
Uzbek Republic, 57

Vereshchagin, famous pictures, 63

Vladmir, Prince of Kieff, 73
Vladimir, proposed visit to, 59, 117
Volga, towns and villages, 59

Weimar Republic, 93, 98
Welfare in industry, 55

Welfare, old people, 74, 117
Winter Palace, 35

Yaroslav, the Wise, 73

Zhitomir, 80
Zhivago, Dr, 20, 55, 56